Reclaimed Wood

A Field Guide

Alan Solomon + Klaas Armster

Photographs by Michel Arnaud

Abrams, New York

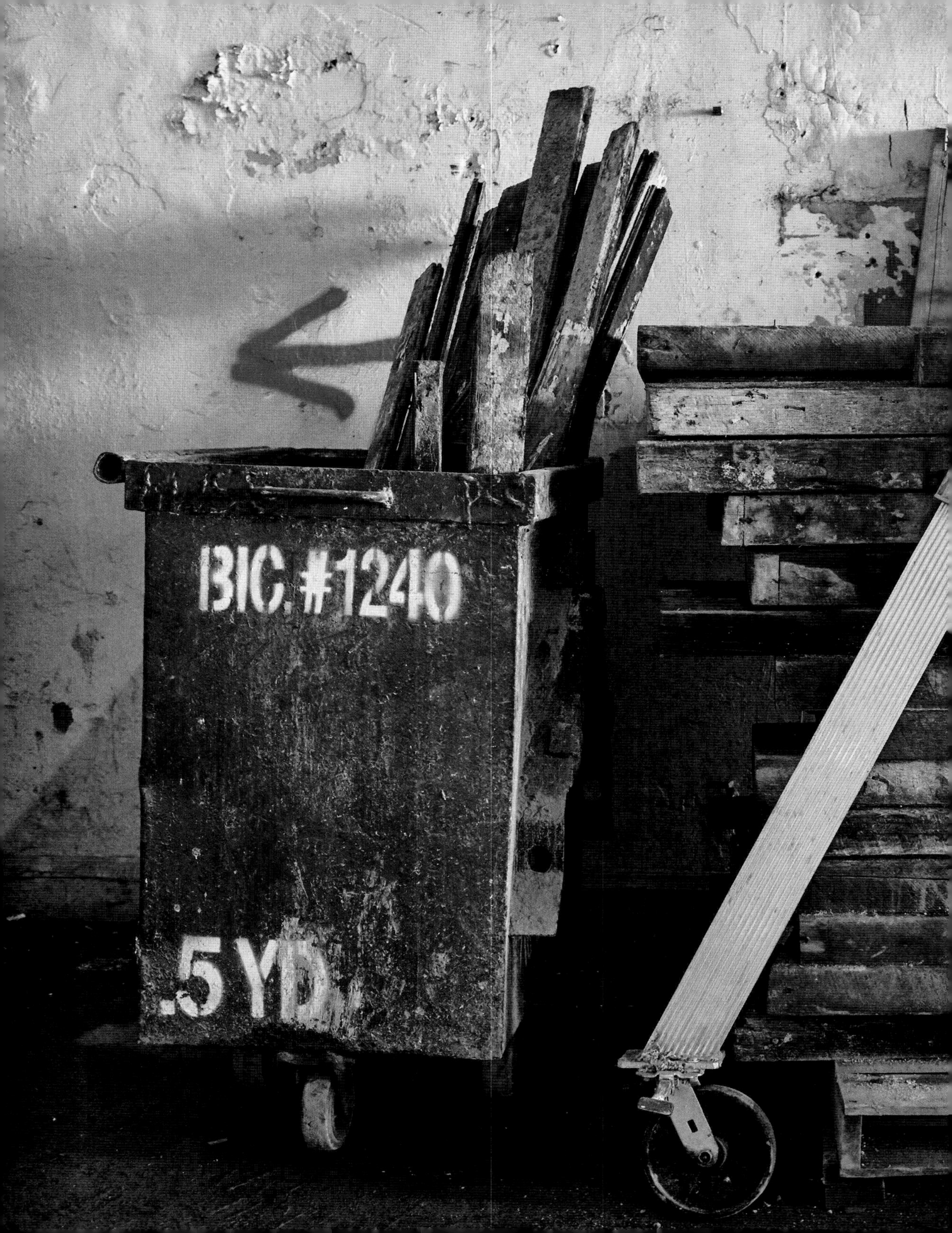
BIC.#1240
.5 YD.

Contents

Foreword

The first American field guide, *How to Know the Wild Flowers*, by Mrs. William Starr Dana, appeared in 1893. Its publication came at the height of logging across North America's virgin forests. The guide was meant to foster an intimacy with nature's small, extraordinary, and often overlooked wildflowers, found as close as "Fifth Avenue . . . in an earth-filled chink of pavement."

Reclaimed Wood is, in some respects, also a field guide. Our survey, however, catalogs a now almost absent feature of the natural world. Today, the virgin forest can be known in America not in the wild but in the exquisite grain and figure, the aged surfaces and human markings, of reclaimed structural lumber. In these pages, we look back, to reveal the history and nature of those timbers, and also forward—to their new use in modern settings and the forests that remain.

The book is a collaborative effort, though we start from different perspectives: as the son of a mill owner and architect, Klaas discovered the beauty and rarity of old woods, and how modern design is brought to life with them. Alan spent a life in salvage and became acquainted with reclaimed woods through his work in historic preservation, and then researched their origins in ancient forests, nineteenth-century logging camps, and old buildings of all kinds.

Our review is broad, and structured around five sources of reclaimed wood—old houses and apartment buildings, barns, industrial buildings, wooden tanks, and what we call "curious and uncommon" structures—but it is an enormous subject that eludes attempts at comprehensiveness. What we do offer is what we know, from a long, deep relation with reclaimed wood, based on our experience in the eastern United States.

—Alan Solomon and Klaas Armster

Nothing
is lost,
everything
is
transformed.

—Antoine-Laurent Lavoisier

<
Eastern white pine stair treads
in a loft in Brooklyn (page 165).

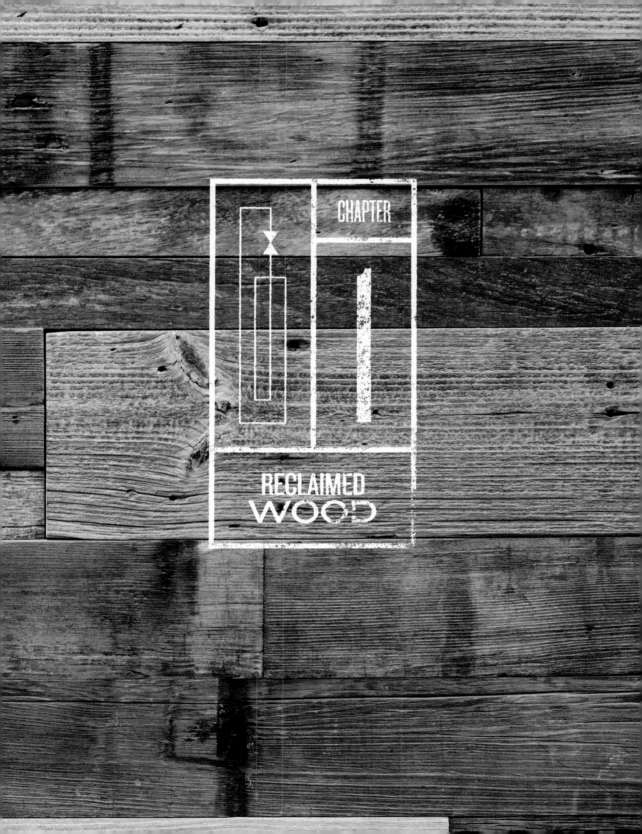

CHAPTER

RECLAIMED
WOOD

The Ages of Wood

For the purposes of this book, reclaimed wood refers to timber predominantly cut from old-growth forests, originally used to build structures in the nineteenth and the early twentieth century and subsequently recovered as lumber to be reused.

For us, the term evokes both a sense of loss—the ancient forests are now largely gone—and a sense of preservation and renewal. The forests reemerge through the demolition process, bearing the marks and color of age and wear, and with a story to tell.

To help guide us, we can distinguish reclaimed wood in several ways: by the age of the wood and its sylvan origins, by the species of tree it came from, and by the type of structure the wood was originally used for. These three elements not only help account for the specific visual qualities of each wood—color, grain, texture, and markings—they also provide meaning in the form of history and sustainability. Together, these elements constitute the allure of reclaimed woods.

First turning our attention to age, we use these broad categories:

Old growth or **virgin** refers to wood that was cut from a mature, naturally established forest, seemingly untouched by human intervention. The lumber from these forests has highly valued qualities—it can be massive, incredibly dense, richly hued, and often all heartwood, free of the lighter outer sapwood that moves water and minerals. These forests, composed of trees that were often hundreds of years old, were plundered, from the late eighteenth century to the mid-twentieth century, to build much of the United States. As a great deal of these old-growth forests have been cut, and nearly all are, thankfully, now off-limits to logging, reclaiming these woods from buildings is the only way not only to access the timber's unique physical characteristics, but also to preserve an essential element of the American landscape. With so many older structures having incorporated what is also now termed *antique wood*, old-growth timber makes up a large volume of reclaimed lumber stock.

Second growth refers to the trees that grew after the old-growth forest had been heavily cut. These trees, too, were used throughout the nineteenth and twentieth centuries, but tended to be younger at the time of logging than old-growth trees, often fifty to more than one hundred years old. Their different growing conditions and less mature ages are inscribed in the figures and grains of the woods—growth rings are broader and less numerous, colors are more muted. Distinguishing old growth from second growth is not always easy, and we sometimes turn from nature to human history for the answers—the nail type, surface patina, saw mark pattern, and age of the structure can help us date the original wood. Second-growth wood, also referred to as *vintage*, is a valuable source of reclaimed material. It tells a story of natural renewal after the intense logging of an earlier era.

<<
Wall installation at City Point, Brooklyn (page 193). Gray barn siding, southeast Asian cargo woods, Coney Island boardwalk, cypress vinegar-tank wood.

<
Old-growth timber has tight growth rings. Longleaf pine sourced at 104 South Street, New York City (built c. 1823). The tree may live to five hundred years.

<

Logging eastern white pine
in northern Wisconsin. Detroit
Photographic Company, c. 1890s.

∧

Second-growth timber is
characterized by wider growth
rings, lighter tone, and softer
wood, relative to old-growth
timber.

Plantation-grown wood comes from trees that were raised to be harvested, just like any other crop. Managed tree farms emerged as a response to the intense logging of the old-growth forests in the late 1800s. First cultivated as saplings in a nursery and then replanted in an artificial forest, these trees are subject to chemical treatments and cut at a relatively young age, and therefore don't develop the dense fibers and complex roots systems of the old-growth trees. As a result, the woods' characteristics are strikingly different from those of old-growth or second-growth woods—paler colors, more frequent knots, and wide, evenly spaced growth rings that resemble the rings of a target at a shooting range. However, these woods have an essential role, primarily in providing wood for stick-frame construction, and also as a necessary alternative, now that old-growth and second-growth logging has largely ceased. A reclaimed-lumber company may increasingly stock reclaimed woods that originated on plantations, but, at this moment, in this book, we are chiefly interested in celebrating and preserving the remaining old-growth woods.

New wood refers herein to a whole slew of material, from shipping pallets and scaffolding planks to a range of manmade boards like plywood. While

Longleaf pine is being regenerated in areas of the South. Most of today's trees—like the fast-growing pines strapped to the back of the flatbed truck—are freshly cut on half-century or less rotations.

we occasionally see these woods at the yard, they are generally recycled as mulch or biofuel. Neither these woods nor woods reclaimed from downed trees and urban logging are part of our project. There is clearly value in the woods' reuse, but they are part of a trade different from ours.

There are many ways that this salvaged and often remanufactured product expresses its value. Reclaimed wood—a natural product—represents a backlash against living in a society where it has become hard to distinguish what is natural and sustainable. With a lot of new wood, there is very little character to draw upon: knots and maybe heartwood and sapwood. Reclaimed wood offers many more dimensions with which to work.

Textures and patterns and tones speak to the wood's life in the forest and in human society, whether it was a threshing floor or a vinegar tank or a factory joist. There is evidence of its place in the history of technology—the cut nail versus a round nail, for instance. Say, "This is wood that was used in a barn," and you immediately call up all sorts of associations with the world of barns. It's story can even be specific to a site or an era, like the Edison maple on page 94.

People often search to describe something special in old wood beyond its material features—an aura that speaks to qualities that don't meet the eye. Closely connected with this is an instinct to rescue neglected wood and put it back to work in modern design.

Reclaimed Up-Close

The character of reclaimed wood is revealed through its surface features, each a clue to its species, age, and use (or abuse). In these visual codes, we can read its story. Here is an overview of common markings.

1
Nail Holes
Nail holes are often ringed with ebonized marks that result from iron dissolving into the surrounding wood fibers. These stains can take the form of brushstrokes or stay tight, as though squeezed out with an eyedropper.

2
Stress cracks
Splits and end checks develop from stresses and seasonal wood movement. The process of expansion and contraction causes micro explosions of wood fibers.

3
Knots
Knots are remnants of encased branches. Their varied forms, sizes, and checking can relate to species and growth. Sometimes a knot may "blow out" or be loose at the perimeter, (as seen here), a sign of a branch that died long before the tree was felled. Knots in wood are often maligned but also express its nature.

4
Impacts
Dents can appear, perhaps the work here of a few drunk hammer blows.

5
Gouges
Gouges signal recent nail removal and may be small or doozies of distress.

6
Grain
The pattern on the surface that results from the configuration of the wood's fibers. Common grain patterns include vertical grain and spiral grain (lower right); open or coarse grain (lower left); and end grain (p. 14/17).

7
Figure
Figure is sometimes interchangeable with grain, but here describes the general appearance of the wood, inclusive of knots, patterns, and other natural features that appear when reclamation shakes off the old surface.

8
Color or tone
The warm browns and silver grays often found in reclaimed wood result from a range of factors, including biological processes in surface cells, the penetration of water bearing minerals and other chemical agents, age, and exposure to sunlight. The white powdery areas are remnants of old lime-based whitewash.

9
Insect tracings
Termites, carpenter ants, and numerous other insects can leave precision holes and other tracings from their headlong rush into a tree.

10
Fungus
Wood may last forever in a dry, cool place. But when wood is moist, fungal decay can set in, leaving holes, rot, or stain on the face of a board.

11
Texture
Texture varies across species and over time and conditions. The feathered texture here is characteristic of white pine. The surface texture of eastern hemlock, on the other hand, is brittle and splintery.

12
Saw marks
Saw-mark patterns indicate the type of mill used and can help in dating wood.

>
clockwise from top left
Eastern white pine with original surface, skip-planed oak barnwood, resurfaced longleaf pine said to be saturated with whale oil, resurfaced wormy chestnut.

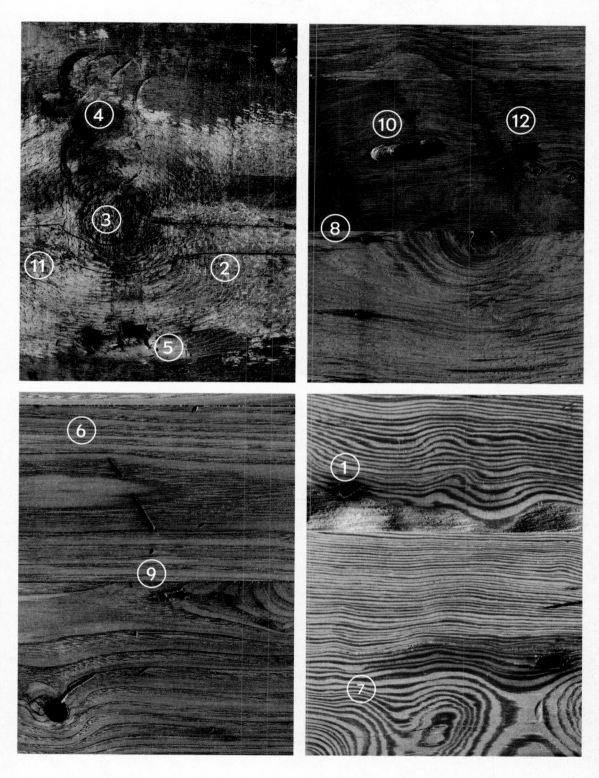

From Secondhand to Reclaimed

To save and salvage seems basic to human nature. Early civilizations undoubtedly left little to waste. Cave dwellers must have tossed broken clubs into the fire. The Bible exhorted: "Beat your swords into plowshares." So while reclaimed wood is not a new thing, our way of using it—that is, treating it as a choice rather than a necessity—is.

The names for it vary. It can be called "used" or "repurposed," "scrap" and "salvaged." In the industry, many names have avoided the suggestion of sustainability and reuse, at least directly, in favor of "antique," "vintage," and "virgin growth."

For hundreds of years, a popular term was "secondhand." It suggested the passing of an object from one human hand to another—central to the idea of reclaimed wood—but demoted it to second.

To the new lumber dealer of the early twentieth century, old wood was both respected and a nuisance. In 1919, the *Southern Lumberman*, a trade journal, reported, "the *second-hand lumber* proposition is something that cannot be waved aside." Mid-century American ads start to list "used lumber"; any glamour has been stripped from the mass-produced commodity. By then, old lumber was being recovered in large volume and offered at a discount for rough work like lining sewers. Builders also incorporated used lumber when new became a critical war resource.

After the war, something else was starting to happen. In the 1950s and early 1960s, magazines like *House Beautiful* featured stories of homeowners who found "beauty in the junkyard," with profiles of interiors that included recovered wood and other materials. Some architects bridging modern and vernacular traditions, like A. Hays Town in Louisiana (page 166) and Jonathan Foote in the Rocky Mountains (page 191), were also beginning to incorporate salvaged wood.

The use of scrap in art goes back to the collages of Pablo Picasso and Georges Braque in 1910. A quarter century later, there were the combines of Robert Rauschenberg, John Chamberlain's welded automobile parts, and Carl Andre's minimalist reclaimed timber sculptures. ("The wood was better before I cut it than after," Andre said. "I did not improve it in any way.") Art had pointed to old things' value as symbols and elevated their aged surfaces.

The origins of today's interest in reclaimed wood can also be traced to the counterculture of the late 1960s and early 1970s. Hippie activists launched voluntary recycling centers and co-ops and scoured used lumber yards and abandoned barns, to build and live as cheaply as possible. Books like *The Whole Earth Catalog* (1968) or *Shelter* by Lloyd Kahn (1970) spread the word.

The growing movement for historical preservation, spurred by events like the destruction of New York's Penn Station (1963), may have also been a factor, as even a raw building material from a demolished structure could be seen to have provenance.

The terms "secondhand" and "used lumber" no longer worked. Wood was being salvaged *and* remanufactured, which explains how the term *reclaimed wood* came into use. It could be made to look rustic or refined, and in the process the history of a specific site was being preserved through modern design. This was something new in the late twentieth century.

Some of the woods had been around for more than a thousand years. They'd come from virgin forests and carried the allure of old buildings. It's a wonder that it took so long for the name to be reclaimed.

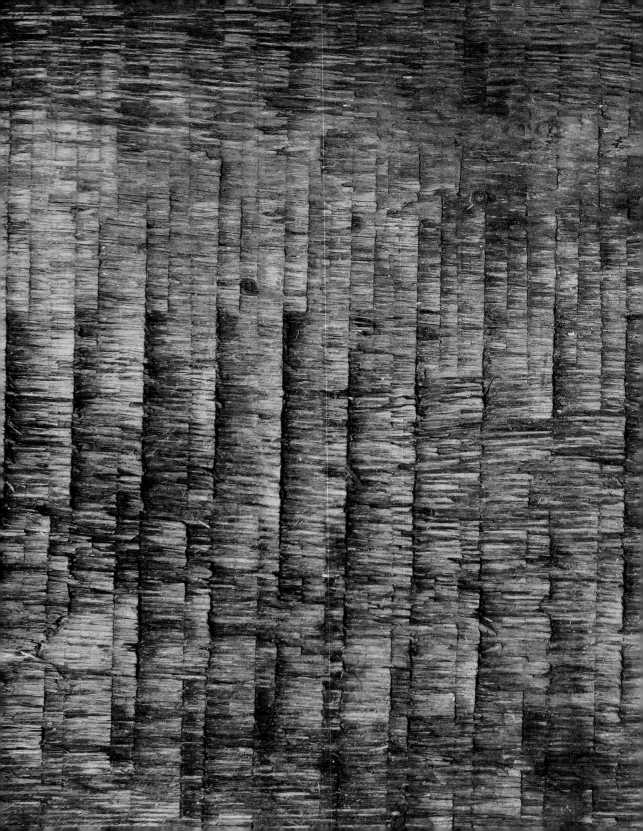

CHAPTER

2

A SHORT
HISTORY
OF WOOD IN
AMERICA

Wood in Great Abundance

There have been many histories written about America's forests, shedding light on their value to the American economy and culture, and describing their remarkable nature. We've come to understand this history, however, through the lens of the woods that are being reclaimed. Seeing old lumber from hundreds of demolished buildings, primarily in the Northeast, we've discovered the species that were used in different eras and followed their paths back to their old-growth forests. Our history of wood in America is informed by this experience and adapted from the best-known works on the subject. It's also a very brief overview, so a few of these wonderful books are listed on page 236 for readers who'd like to explore the subject further.

Some of the wood we're now reclaiming was in the virgin forests, growing on American soil before Christopher Columbus arrived. Native Americans had long been clearing land with fire for hunting and farming, and venerating the spirits of trees, especially the eastern white pine, or Tree of Peace.

It's hard to overestimate the role of the forests in everyday life in North America, but, for the first Europeans, wood was of little importance to their hopes and dreams. The Pilgrims of 1620 sailed to Plymouth to gain religious freedom. The early Dutch explorers were looking for a passage to another place, farther east. The English who settled Jamestown, Virginia, in 1607 were in search of financial return, preferably gold. What they all found, revered, and then exploited was trees. The first arrivals witnessed the virgin forests rising out of the sea as they came closer to shore. In his journal of Henry Hudson's 1609 voyage, Robert Juet admired the trees on the banks of the river that would be named for the explorer: "goodly Oakes, and Wal-nut trees, and Chestnut trees, Ewe trees, and trees of sweet wood in great abundance." The forests were dense and, for the most part, impenetrable by horse.

These forests that the Pilgrims stumbled upon provoked fear. Many of the *Mayflower* passengers died the first winter, unable to make effective use of the wood for shelter. For Dutch settlers in New Amsterdam, they offered the greatest supply of timber they'd ever seen. In the 1620s, the advanced Dutch sawmills—technology that helped drive the Dutch Golden Age—were deployed to an early logging site: the backwoods of Manhattan Island (overleaf). The Dutch settlers' water-powered sawmill was located near today's Central Park, along the Saw-kill (Dutch for "sawmill creek"), producing lumber that rounded out shipments of beaver pelts and other goods to Europe. Many of the old buildings standing in New York City are framed, it was a wonder to discover, with lumber that's old enough to have grown at the site when it was a virgin forest.

<<
Pre-Civil War Northeast softwood board, with up-and-down saw marks.

<
Giant Redwood Trees of California. Painting by Albert Bierstadt, c. 1874.

The Eastern Forests
Early 1700s–1850

During the early colonial era, the eastern white pine was the predominant wood, and the most versatile for building. The forests are gone now, but we see the wood in pre–Civil War commercial structures, like the Classical revival

MAP
SHOWING THE
NATURAL DIVISIONS
OF THE
NORTH AMERICAN FORESTS
EXCLUSIVE OF MEXICO
Prepared under the direction of
C. S. SARGENT SPECIAL AGENT

ALEUTIAN ISLANDS

Julius Bien & Co. lith. N.Y.

warehouses that lined the edge of lower Manhattan. And the first street north of Wall Street, at Manhattan's tip, is Pine Street. The white pine was the tallest tree in the eastern United States, and it was prized for ship masts, which were key to naval power. King George I enacted a law in 1723 to mark the best pine trees, with a blaze called the King's Broad Arrow carved into the bark, to reserve them for the British Navy.

The colonists often cut the the trees anyway, and the rebel loggers were an early sign of the revolution to come. A skirmish in the backwoods of New Hampshire dubbed the White Pine War or the Pine Tree Riot was part of the lead-up to the Boston Tea Party. And the eastern white pine was featured on one of the first colonial flags, a symbol of democracy, where "everyone is extraordinary and a dime-a-dozen," like pine. The flag flew at the Battle of Bunker Hill, it's said, and shows up in John Trumbull's well-known paintings of the event (overleaf).

As the young country got under way, lumber production increased steadily, and the forests seemed vast and limitless. To pioneers, trees were an obstacle to be cleared with sweat, skill, and strength. The demand for lumber regularly spiked higher. It was needed for everything from cabins, barns, and factories to carts, fuel, and mine shafts. Logging that had begun close to waterways moved inland. Forests fell and were sent downriver to build the growing cities

<
Map Showing the Natural Divisions of the North American Forests, 1884. The main divisions are the northeastern pine forests, the vast deciduous forests in the center of the country, the coastal pine forest in the South, and the Pacific forests in the West.

∨
View of New Amsterdam. Painting by Johannes Vingboons, 1664. A mill appears in the upper left corner. Early Dutch settlers launched commercial lumbering on the continent.

NIEUW AMSTERDAM OFTE NUE NIEUW IORX OPT TEYLANT MAN

of the East Coast. A scant amount of the massive numbers of trees used still resides in surviving old buildings.

In 1840, about a third of the country's lumber came from New York State, which benefited from its northern forests and the Erie Canal. Much of the balance came from other northeastern states—assessed at more than 1.5 billion board feet total, not including all the woods cut by farmers for barns and other uses.

With the onset, in the 1860s, of the Second Industrial Revolution, the logging industry was able to adopt improvements in engineering and machinery, from refinements in metal saw blades to the spiked shoes worn by the daredevil river men. Log trains were replacing river drives. Only the ax maintained a seemingly timeless presence, with regional variations on its bold and elegant form. In the sawmills, steam was also replacing water power. Circular saws grew in size, and up-and-down gang saws could cut logs into multiple boards at a pass, up to forty thousand board feet a day, enough to frame a few multi-story row buildings. In fact, building lots were in part determined by the size of the available lumber, then roughly twenty feet in length. The result is the long, unbroken board lengths of reclaimed woods we see today, allowing them to be made into floors, paneling, and furniture.

"Get the wood out!" became an increasingly common shout in the backwoods. Meanwhile, a small circle of writers raised an alarm about the intense logging. The poet Lydia Sigourney—"the sweet singer of Hartford" was the most widely read American woman writer of the early 1800s— wrote the poem "Fallen Forests" in 1830. The verse cut like a woodsman's ax against what she called "man's warfare on the trees," which she witnessed moving across Upstate New York and into the American heartland: "The hills and vales covered with stately and immense trunks that . . . lie like soldiers, when battle is done." Her hope is that "a far-reaching mind will spare here and there, the time-honored tree."

But the forests continued to fall. In 1869, William H. H. Murray (*Adventures in the Wilderness; or, Camp-Life in the Adirondacks*) despaired: "Wherever the axe sounds, the pride and beauty of the forest disappear. A lumbered district is the most dreary and dismal region the eye of man ever beheld. . . . The streams and trout-pools are choked with saw-dust . . . The rivers are blockaded with 'booms' . . . bones, offal, horse-manure, and all the débris of a deserted lumbermen's village is strewn around. The hills and shores are littered with rotten wood, in all stages of decomposition."

The Great Lakes States

1850–1900

By the mid-1800s, the logging industry spread to the Great Lakes states of Michigan, Wisconsin, and Minnesota, after the pines of the Northeast, which once seemed limitless, were about gone. A Maine congressman lamented in 1852, "the stalwart sons of Maine are marching away by the scores and hundreds to the piney woods of the Northwest." That same year, Congressman Ben Eastman of Wisconsin boasted, "Upon the rivers which . . . empty themselves into Lake Michigan, there are interminable forests of pines, sufficient to supply all the wants of the citizens . . . for all time to come."

That was also the year eighteen-year-old Frederick Weyerhaeuser arrived in New York City from Germany. The future timber mogul would be a

<
The Death of General Warren at the Battle of Bunker's Hill, 17 June 1775. Painting by John Trumbull, 1815–31. The Pine Tree Flag appears in the upper left corner and is said to have flown at the battle.

>
The great lumber raft sent by sea from Nova Scotia to New York. Harper's Weekly, 1893. The raft, comprising 4.5 million feet of lumber, was towed from Two Rivers, Canada, to Newtown Creek in Brooklyn.

THE RAFT BEFORE LAUNCHING

transitional figure, as logging became increasingly industrialized. After stints at a number of jobs, he headed west and soon became a partner in a small sawmill, which would be his life's direction. He had set his sights on white pine, which was still the most versatile timber, because it is large, durable, stable, and decay-resistant. In the view of lumbermen like Weyerhaeuser, white pine could be felled by the grove, making for economies of scale. And the logs floated well. But Weyerhaeuser's business became a logjam. All the working parts of the industry, from stump to mill, were generally separate businesses. It was a chaotic trade, but Weyerhaeuser mastered it by seeking to understand the whole network. Unlike other mill owners, he went deep into Wisconsin's Chippewa Valley to the source of the wood. And although he was happy with the simple life of the camp and the backwoods, there were problems that needed solving downriver, where hostilities and rivalries made business hazardous. He formed the Mississippi River Logging Company, which established a way for rival companies to coordinate work, and he quickly managed to double production. That increased security and economies of scale all around. His lumber production expanded until the *New York Times* declared that Weyerhaeuser "came close to a monopoly of the great industry."

The country was growing rapidly as immigrants arrived by the millions to be remade as American citizens. Demand for lumber continued to rise, and Chicago replaced Albany as the leading port for it. The mill towns that began to spread throughout the Great Lakes area were said to look as if they were made of sawdust. The region's vast networks of rivers and lakes made it possible to get wood to metropolitan areas in the eastern United States and to build out the prairie states with its white pine. Meanwhile, in the Northeast, the volume of white pine was diminishing, and its place was being taken by other species like hemlock, spruce, balsam fir, and red pine. Just about any old-growth tree large enough to yield "saw logs" felt the ax. This diversity of species and wood grains is evident below the aged brown surface of reclaimed wood from demolished late nineteenth- and early twentieth-century apartment houses. By the latter half of the 1800s, the assault on the forests of the Great Lakes states was coming to an end. The South was next.

The Southern United States

1840–1910

Between 1866 (when the Civil War came to an end) and 1910, logging in the South rose from 1.5 billion to 15.5 billion board feet a year. There, longleaf pine forests ran from western Texas to the Florida Panhandle and as far north as Chesapeake Bay. Longleaf, which differs in look and qualities from the white pine that was popular in the North, had been exploited since the early 1800s, but it wasn't until northern timber companies invaded, with capital and technology, after the Civil War that logging volumes rose to staggering levels. The Second Industrial Revolution accelerated in the late 1800s, and, despite the period's strong association with steel, its architecture still relied on stone and wood, predominantly southern longleaf pine. The industrial buildings

^
*The Lumber District of
Chicago—View from the
West Side Waterworks.
Harper's Weekly*, 1883.
Illustration by
Charles Graham.

framed during this era continue to generate the largest volume of reclaimed wood today, and virtually all the timbers, some as large as twenty inches square, that we find in them are longleaf pine. Southern pine was shipped up the Mississippi to northern cities; it went downriver to ships docked at eastern ports from northern Florida to the Carolinas; and it traveled out of southern ports on the Gulf of Mexico, where there was also trade in bald cypress, which grew into massive trees in the delta area below Baton Rouge and in southern swamps.

The southern landscape furthered efficiencies in the logging industry, and improvements in technology continued with new rail networks and steam-powered saws. Here, the "company town" made its contribution to productivity. Longleaf is well known for its density, which results from hard resins—but the resins stick to machinery parts and necessitate frequent cleaning and blade changes. But the wood's density was only a minor stumbling block. The virtues of the wood—size, strength, and hardness— were too many to impede its use. Far away from the new, massive southern mills, southern longleaf pine was rapidly winning acceptance across the country. But it also stayed local, to rebuild New Orleans, Richmond, Washington, DC, and outlying mills and factories.

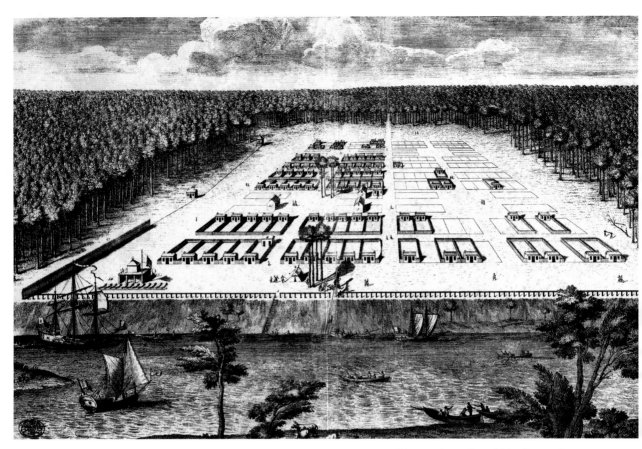

The work crews were said to consist of formerly enslaved black people and white small-farm owners. They worked in segregated groups, in the southern towns where longleaf was being heavily logged.

By 1900, Louisiana was a hub. Construction of a mill often marked the establishment of a new town, as it did in Bogalusa, Louisiana, in 1907. The mill was owned by the Great Southern Lumber Company, whose name still turns up in the faded stamps on old timber. But many mill towns across the South were soon abandoned, the longleaf pine no longer their "pulsing heart," in the words of R. D. Forbes in the early 1900s. The mills, Forbes wrote, were "'sawed out.'"

The Pacific Northwest

Late 1800s–1940

The wave of logging that got its start with settlers in the East during the 1600s, that moved to the Great Lakes states in the mid-1800s, and that swept deep into the southern United States later in the nineteenth century, finally leaped over the Great Plains to the Pacific Northwest. The pattern of logging there looks much the same as elsewhere, but the region's landscape and story are strikingly different.

Even for the logging industry, the terrain was challenging, with poor soils, steep slopes, and heavy rains. It's easy, however, to understand the lumbermen's zeal for the Douglas fir and redwood, given their remarkable sizes.

For most of the nineteenth century, the Pacific Northwest had been largely isolated from the main lumber markets, which other regions could serve at cheaper cost. Only at Puget Sound, Humboldt Bay, and, later, San Francisco were there accessible harbors. The overseas cargo trade helped supplement the income of the loggers, who primarily cut and dealt in so-called Oregon pine (another name for Douglas fir). Then, in mid-century, the redwoods were discovered.

As the story goes, a mining company worker in Calaveras County, California, was tracking a wounded grizzly bear and was led into a grove of giant sequoias. When he rushed back to tell the men at camp what he'd seen, no one believed him. Tall tales about the wilderness weren't uncommon. Nevertheless, he brought others to the grove the next day, and news of the extraordinary sequoias spread. There were soon plans to fell a giant tree for the 1853 New York World's Fair. It took five men more than three weeks to cut it down. Ultimately, it was destroyed by a fire while awaiting shipment. The stump remains in the Calaveras State Park. The redwood, the king of trees, had entered the popular imagination, although it was less versatile than other woods from the region and found fewer uses.

In the Northeast, we tend not to see Douglas fir in buildings until the early to mid-twentieth century (page 162). The flow of lumber from closer markets in the South, and higher transport costs for shipping from the Pacific Northwest, impeded Douglas fir's spread east for some time.

Even the completion of the transcontinental Northern Pacific Railway in 1883 did not open up trade between eastern and western states as much as had been expected. But the railroad brought more people west, and it was just a matter of time before the forests received a stampede of new timber barons. Before the large companies moved in, western operations were said to be more peculiar and wasteful than operations elsewhere in the country. Oregon, for example, had large animal teams, and loggers cut from springboards ten feet off the ground. But lumbering in Oregon, Washington, and California would be transformed by continuously improving technology and methods, and by the Klondike Gold Rush of 1897 and the resulting building boom in Seattle.

As in other regions, in the Pacific Northwest timber companies went after the most commercially viable species, such as Douglas fir and cedar, and doubled back for other trees like western hemlock and Sitka spruce, which we see in buildings from mid-century or later. The Pacific Northwest has actively renewed its forests with smaller trees and continues to be a leading source of lumber in the nation. There's certain to be ongoing volumes of these regional woods reclaimed in the future.

<

A View of Savannah as it stood the 29th of March 1734. This print, based on a drawing by Peter Gordon, includes a rare depiction of the dense longleaf forests that extended through the South.

Reclaimed Forests

There were pressures, regional and national, to restrain the logging industry, but preservation efforts centered on the most extraordinary spaces. In 1864, with the Civil War raging, President Abraham Lincoln signed the Yosemite Grant Act, setting aside Yosemite and the Mariposa Big Tree Grove for "public use, resort, and recreation . . . inalienable for all time." Eventually, the danger of total exploitation of the forests, and the consequences of their destruction, aroused politicians, like Theodore Roosevelt, and environmentalists, like Gifford Pinchot, who became the first chief of the US Forest Service in 1905, to launch the conservation movement and establish the practice of silviculture, leading to the work of sustainable forestry today.

As iron started to replace timber in heavy industry, and as farming shifted to cheaper western lands, the forests started to come back, though dramatically altered in scale and composition. It can be hard to imagine what the virgin stands that yielded old-growth lumber were like. Today, they're scarce.

It's said that, by the early 1900s, more than one trillion board feet of lumber had been felled. It was burned for fuel, made into buildings and ships and vehicles of all kinds, processed into wood pulp or pine pitch or naval stores (when the trees weren't stripped for leather tanning), cut into countless rail ties and staves for barrels and tanks, assembled into fencing for lands from which it was cleared, used to line sewers and bridge caissons, nailed into crates and boxes, and turned, carved, and molded into wheels, gears, floors, bookshelves, stair parts, and other goods. In our times, every old-growth board is a portal to lost virgin forests.

Our Logging Heritage

Ever since 1607, when settlers arrived in Jamestown, Virginia, a land of "goodly tall trees," Americans have been logging. Prior to that, Native Americans also felled trees, though by girdling the bases with fire. The early American lumberjacks were generally held in high regard, as theirs was a hard life. Most loggers who stayed with the trade were rough laborers with powerful capacity for the work and the endurance to survive harsh winters in the wilderness. But, though it was dangerous and grueling, the work could be immensely satisfying. America and its cities would not exist without the backwoods lumberjack and his ax.

Given the often romantic view of the lumberjack, it's easy to overlook the larger crew and the varied skills needed in a full-scale logging operation. The so-called timber cruisers were (and still are) the first to head into a forest on

Who robbed
the woods,
The trusting
woods? . . .
What will
the solemn
hemlock,
What will the
fir-tree say?

—Emily Dickinson, *Nature XVII*

<
*Felling Cedar Tree Thirty
Miles East of Seattle,
76 feet in Circumference,
18 in From Ground.*
Photograph by Darius Kinsey,
1906.

^
Riverside logging camp,
Michigan, 1899.

>>
Log boom, possibly the
Puget Mill Co., Port Ludlow,
Washington. Photograph
by John D. Cross, c. 1900.
A log boom in a river or
lake contains floating logs.

foot. They scout out timberlands with the right yield, examine transport routes, anticipate obstacles, and foresee all the logistics. The lumber kings put a lot of faith in the cruisers' work.

The camp boss put the plan into motion, lined up the supplies, and filled the jobs. This person needed to be a careful manager, as, once in the wilderness, there's no going back for provisions. You'd also have filers to keep the saws sharp, and a blacksmith. There were scalers, experts at measuring the sizes and volumes of logs—another specialty of the trade, and subject to local rules. Swampers cleared roads; cant dog men moved the de-limbed harvest with pole spikes; sled tenders and teamsters harnessed oxen, mules, or horses to pyramidal loads, grunting them into clearings or down skid rows; nimble-footed river men drove the timber downstream to the mills. The list of jobs seems to go on and on. There was the cook—the best of them had celebrity-chef status. And, lastly, there was the camp clerk. Bookkeeping is said to be underappreciated.

> A man was
> famous
> according
> as he had
> lifted up
> axes upon
> the
> thick trees.
>
> —Psalms 74:5

After dinner in a logging camp, there were the expected pastimes—pipe smoking, card playing, and spinning yarns. There were the maintenance tasks—washing, mending, and patching clothes; drying mittens and greasing boots; sharpening axes. On Sundays, a lumberjack might dictate a letter to a person in the group who could write, gather spruce gum, and refresh the hemlock boughs of his bed. He'd fish and hunt in the woods. Some lumberjacks got out of hand at the end of the season, carousing in small towns. Music and songs passed from camp to camp, some becoming traditions. This popular refrain sounds like a summer camp alma mater:

The music of our burnished ax shall make the woods resound
And many a lofty ancient Pine will tumble to the ground.
At night round our shanty fire, we'll sing while rude winds blow.
We'll range the wild woods over, while a'lumbering we go.

^
Swampers carving out a mountain road. Photograph by William T. Clarke, 1897–98.

>
Logger, crosscut saw and felled tree. Photograph by Darius Kinsey, c. 1915.

42

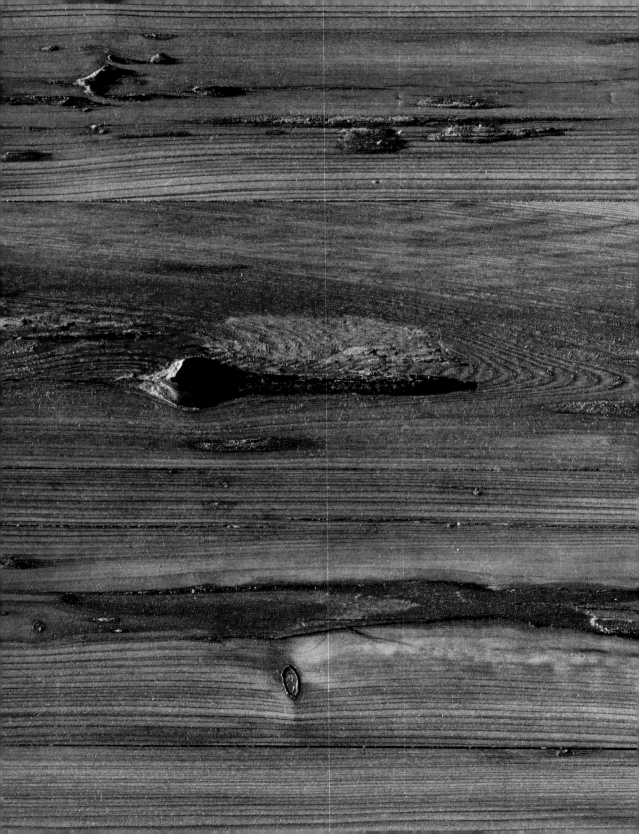

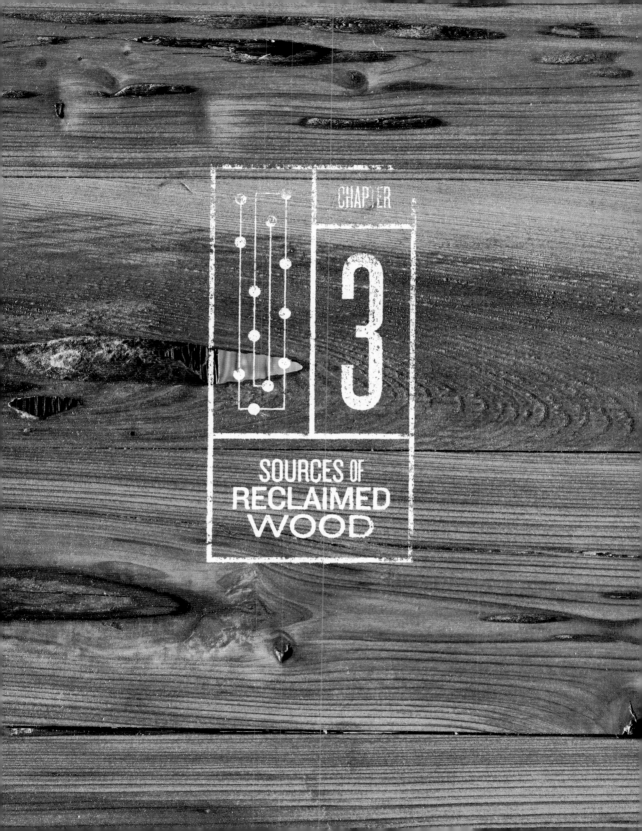

CHAPTER

3

SOURCES OF
RECLAIMED
WOOD

Old Houses and Apartment Buildings

All sources of reclaimed lumber are diverse in their species, but old houses are the most unassuming. That goes for the woods covered here, with the exception of one hardwood—wormy chestnut.

Old houses were usually framed with old-growth conifers—softwoods that generally serve as construction lumber. Through the eras, the grade can change, from old growth to second growth. But the woods are similar in their dimensions—about three inches thick and eight to twelve inches wide, depending on the housing type. And, in one way, the diverse old house woods are identical: Their rough-sawn surfaces turn shades of brown.

The label "old" is broadly applied to pre-1910 houses. Most that get demolished were built in the late nineteenth century, but the oldest house included in this book, near our Connecticut sawmill, dates from 1688 (opposite and pages 50–51). It's framed with white oak, suspected to have been sawn at a new water-powered mill in the area. Later-era apartment houses (page 49) would have been framed with a mix of softwood joists, all displaying the period's rough circular-saw pattern; the wood is likely red spruce sent down the Hudson River, white pine out of the ports of Maine, balsam fir that thrived in Nova Scotia, or eastern hemlock sent by rail from the Black Forest of Pennsylvania—or more than one. A late nineteenth-century urban row house can reveal a mix of woods, as diverse as the immigrants it sheltered. In cities and towns across the United States, the species might be different,

<<
The distinctive holes in pecky cypress are caused by an airborne fungus that enters damaged trees and eats away at the heartwood. This panel has an oil finish.

<
An old house in East Hartford, Connecticut, dated to 1688 (page 50).

>
Tenement house interior. Detroit Publishing Company, c. 1900–10.

but they would be regional softwoods all the same. For a long time, that's the way it was done, until industrialization, economies of scale, streamlined transport, and scientific forestry consolidated the trade.

Chestnut can be a treasure within old houses. It is hallowed among reclaimed woods. Words fail. The chestnut was devastated by an early twentieth-century blight, which accounts for some of the reverence paid to the tree. It was also a commonly used wood, historically, and it is regularly salvaged, though growing scarcer. Single-family houses, along with barns, are its only source.

I think that mysterious things happen in familiar places. We don't always need to run to the other end of the world.

—Saul Leiter, photographer

^
A turn-of-the-century lumberyard.

>
The La Grange apartment building, Newark, New Jersey, built c. 1900, photographed after a fire destroyed the top two floors. The building is still in use.

The Oldest Houses

Reclamation is often a low priority in preservation. That's the case with the oldest houses. The top priority is to preserve the house where it stands, or to preserve parts of the house. Only if that's not possible is the house dismantled and sent to a reclaimed-lumber company.

That's a last resort for preservationists like Steve Bielitz. "A lot of people are pickers, and they just save elements of houses," he says. "I try to save a whole house. As soon as you change the length of a beam, or you do not use the mortise and tenon arrangement as [it was] originally intended, then you're changing it completely."

When more complete preservation is not possible, Bielitz tries to reuse the house in another context. For instance, he recycled some of the hand-planed sheathing of a 1760 house

in Glastonbury, Connecticut, in another house of the same period. He sold the frame to a gentleman in Coventry, a town to the east, who carefully used all the material to create an addition to an 1870s house. Other pieces may go to old houses that need parts.

In their forms and patinas, even parts of old houses are evocative. They can be worn by a century of smoke from the hearth, or bear the roman numerals of carpenters' marks or saw patterns from the town's first water-powered mill. Every part in these "first period" homes retains some of the psychic energy that's in that wood. The 1688 house that is featured here may appear to be leaning, as if close to collapse. But soon after we entered, we saw that it's built like a battleship. This house has been preserved and will eventually be moved to a new site.

>
The house was framed with white oak and built out with white pine planks, eight to twenty inches in width. A dendrochronologist used the oak to date the house.

Northeast Softwoods

Picea rubens (red spruce), *Pinus strobus* (white pine),
Pinus resinosa (red pine), *Abies balsamea* (balsam fir),
Tsuga canadensis (hemlock)

Regional conifers like red spruce, white and red pine, balsam fir, and hemlock (old advertisements use the term white woods for these woods, and they tend to age to similar patina) are typically found together in old row houses and apartment buildings. Pine (page 82) predominated for structural joists in earlier houses, eventually overtaken by red spruce. The red spruce joists in the rough are three inches thick on average, and up to twelve inches wide. The untouched aged surface is brown and rough-sawn. Resurfaced, it is creamy to light brown, and even-grained—and a pleasing backdrop for its natural and distressed qualities. Knots can be frequent, with the occasional nail hole and stress crack.

The name spruce refers to the tree's reddish-brown bark, favored by porcupines. But for humans, spruce was practically a backwoods general store, offering spruce beer, spruce gum, and spruce pudding. Since it is soft, strong, flexible, and light, spruce wood was used on the first of the Wright brothers' planes. It is also an ideal tonal wood: Although it's been regarded as the lowest-value reclaimed wood, spruce is the highest-valued for a Stradivarius violin.

Habitat
Northeastern United States to Nova Scotia. Mountain regions in association with various hardwoods. Also forms homogeneous woods.

Reuse
Architectural joists, flooring, cladding, furniture.

Surfaces
Original: mid-range browns, circular-saw marks. Resurfaced: pale to light brown heartwood, even-grained, knots can break in distinctive patterns, dark nail holes.

note
As indicated in captions, the wood panels illustrated in this chapter have been left in their original condition; skip-planed, where some features of the original surface remain; or resurfaced, where the original surface of the wood has been completely planed away. Unless otherwise noted, the panels are either unfinished or have a clear coat.

∧
A wrecked Wright brothers plane, College Park Aviation Field, Maryland. Photograph by Harris & Ewing, 1911.

>
Northeast softwood, original surface

< Northeast softwood, resurfaced

^
A room in the Gothic
apartment house, Boston,
built c. 1900 and demolished
for the redevelopment of
the North End. Photograph
by Cervin Robinson, 1959.

>
White pine, resurfaced
Pinus strobus

>>
Red pine, resurfaced
Pinus resinosa

American Chestnut

Castanea dentata

In 1904, a ship carrying Japanese chestnut trees arrived in the port of Albany, New York. The trees were carrying a fungus new to the Western Hemisphere. The blight it unleashed on the American chestnut was soon discovered on the grounds of the New York Zoological Society (where the Bronx Zoo stands today). By 1940, virtually all the American chestnuts, lacking the resistance of their Japanese counterparts, had been eradicated.

Besides being one of the most common hardwoods in the eastern United States, chestnut was among the most beloved. "Queen of the American Forest," it was called. Chestnut festivals, where children gathered the tree's nuts for roasting over open fires, were popular. On rich soils, a mature chestnut could grow to more than twenty-five feet in diameter. So, at the time of the blight, farmers and builders had the luxury of sawing the dying trees into cheap barn and house lumber, fence posts,

and furniture. Its handsome grain and unusual appearance, from being riddled with worm holes, has gained it a following today among connoisseurs of salvaged wood.

American chestnut is still available as wood recovered from houses and barns. Its sometimes massive trunks were friendly to work and use. Chestnut has an open oak-like grain and warm hardwood tones. The insect holes that lend it the name wormy chestnut mix with occasional nail holes, stress cracks, and other marks of age. Because of its relative rarity, reclaimed chestnut is expensive and a bit of a holy grail. A batch's reclaimed surface can vary significantly in color, condition, and level of "worminess," so due diligence is needed in its acquisition. The rarity of chestnut and its unique qualities make it almost exclusively a resurfaced or heavily skip-planed material for a range of applications. There also seems to be no level of distress that justifies tossing this extremely rare species.

Tree About 100 feet high and 3 to 4 feet in diameter (and sometimes up to 8, 10, or even 15 feet). In forests, it has a columnar trunk. Pale green, densely spiny cupules. Edible fruits (chestnuts).

Habitat Interior of eastern North America (formerly).

Reuse Floors, cladding, picture frames.

Surfaces Resurfaced: light to medium brown heartwood, coarse grain, light to frequent worm hole pattern.

VIEWS OF THE SAME TREE, TAKEN ON THREE SUCCESSIVE YEARS, 1909, 1910, AND 1911 RESPECTIVELY. WYNCOTE, PA.
[The branches have been cut off as fast as they were killed. The tree will die this summer (1912).]

< Illustration from *Chestnut Tree Blight*, USDA publication, 1912.

> American wormy chestnut, resurfaced *Castanea dentata*

∧
American wormy chestnut,
river dam
Castanea dentata
Over decades underwater, this
wood's open pores absorbed
fresh-water minerals, creating
an ethereal blue-gray tone.

>
American wormy chestnut,
resurfaced
Castanea dentata

Barns

Barnwood is often what comes to mind when we think about reclaimed wood. There's a romance to barns, such that even woods from other sources are finished to be a stand-in for its allure. Barns remain across America, in use or abandoned, but the pace of their removal has accelerated, as the trend for using reclaimed woods has taken hold. Barns (the word comes from the Old English term for "a place to store barley") have existed for thousands of years, and they conjure reverence and nostalgia for a simpler life, close to the land and nature—even if we're not breathing the fresh country air, mixed with the smells of hay, manure, and the restless farm animals.

Until recent times, the whole barn was often built of wood. There are interior wall divisions and heavy plank flooring, called threshing-floor boards, and there are the barn siding and all the structural timbers. Since barns were typically built using trees in the vicinity, and occasionally ones cleared to make space for the barn, they may contain a variety of species. The principal wood is oak, but you find beech, hickory, elm, maple, birch, and chestnut, and often a rarity or two. Farmers could overbuild and be indiscriminate in their wood use.

Barnwood texture almost always includes ax marks, known as "hewn" marks, as well as saw-mark patterns. The more heavily textured the barnwood is, the more "character" it is said to possess, at least by rustic sentimentalists. To a builder and historian, however, a cleaner ax cut is more authentic, representing a skilled and forceful hand and allowing the subtle visual effects on the wood's surface to be seen.

The history of a barn or its site is often lost. The same is happening to its architectural style, as the barn is reduced to an icon. A few notable styles are the Appalachian overhung-loft barn, the New York Dutch barn, and the

<
A tobacco barn in the Connecticut Valley.

v
Barn siding: shades of gray.

prairie corn barn. The function that determined the form of a barn varied: There were dairy, tobacco, and hay barns; corncribs and milk houses; and forge and wagon barns.

Barn dismantlers may specialize in the trade. Their work is a world apart from demolition. There may be a gun in the back of the cab. A common method in barn teardowns is to make some strategic cuts and remove connecting plates along the rafters. Then a couple of cables are run from the back to the front—sometimes ninety feet or more in the large bank barns—and the barn is hooked to the back of a pickup. Then you just give the cables a tug—maybe hit the barn a couple of times—until it collapses and sends up a lot of dust.

The work involves long hours, low pay, and economic uncertainty. About half of the structure becomes waste—too rotted, small, or damaged to salvage. Most barns are "packed full of junk that people threw in for years if they weren't farming," says barn dismantler Raine Dubel. "The stuff they got now on *American Pickers* we just used to scrap—vintage feed bags, old hand tools, tin toys, a lot of cool hinges, a 1930s car hood, and a great collection of lightning rods."

The beauty of wood in the state of pleasing decay is one of Nature's special masterpieces, so remarkable in its composition—grains and knots and shades of weathered gray—that it could be framed and hung just as any modern painting is.

—Eric Sloane,
The Age of Barns (1966)

<
Barn, Boundary County, Idaho.
Photograph by Dorothea Lange,
1939.

^
Dutch barn, Lancaster County,
Pennsylvania. Photograph
by Arthur Rothstein, 1941.

>
Barn in a valley back of Mission
San Jose, Santa Clara County,
California. Photograph
by Dorothea Lange, 1939.

Barns of Many Colors + Textures

An old barn may feel like a unity, but every part of it takes on its own qualities up close, with varied colors and textures determined by species, age, use, or cut (saw or ax). Each surface seems to project the ruckus and tranquility of the place; whether in shades of gray, rustic brown, or the flecked paint of siding. Brown barnwood is the most readily available. Red is the most elusive. Due to scarcity and demand, reproductions have multiplied. If painted barn siding—usually in red or white—is found, it's best to seal it, as it may predate the phasing out of lead-based paint.

^
Hewn oak
Quercus rubra, Quercus alba

>
clockwise from top left
Original surface oak barnwood, red barn siding, oak threshing floor, pine or hemlock gray barnwood.

Sources of Reclaimed Wood

American Oak

Quercus rubra (red oak), *Quercus alba* (white oak),
Quercus viginiana (southern live oak)

Oak is the most common hardwood on the planet. In early America, oak was indispensable to shipbuilding, and in 1823 the Navy commissioned *The Timber Merchant's Guide*, a short book on the subject. Its author, Peter Guillet, sounded a prescient alarm: "When we consider the progressive devastation committed upon the vast forests of this country—that, if the present course be pursued, they must in time entirely disappear—the necessity of taking prohibitory measures for their preservation, must be obvious to every man of intelligence." As plentiful as it is, oak is now at a fraction of its early volume. Dendrochronologist Ed Cook at Columbia University suspects that global warming may also be at work in the significantly lower population of white oak.

Oak is also the most common reclaimed hardwood, primarily from barns and a couple of specialty sources, like barrels once used to store whiskey. Barns yield a range of salvaged forms, including siding, timbers, joists, stall divisions, and the massive threshing-floor boards—the central animal walk and work surface that is sometimes resurrected with wear and distress, lodged bits of hay, and, perhaps, horse piss and insect tracings. Each structural element is distinct in form, texture, wear, and coloration. And every barn is different.

Hand-hewn or ax-sawn timber would be an extreme example of a textured surface. Other structural timbers display saw marks. Nails, metal fasteners, or characteristic or unusual joinery cuts are present. Reclaimed oak is often celebrated for these hard-knocks and weathered textures. But resurfaced oak reveals hidden qualities. When planed smooth, the bare wood shows aged hues, and stress cracks, nail holes, and checked knots are highlighted.

Barn oak is a mix of red and white wood. Sorting for all white oak generally commands a premium. But given oak's rustic original surface, it's hard to see why sorting matters; even when it's skip-planed and resurfaced, differences can be hard to detect. But carefully chosen raw materials can produce different looks, and price discrepancies are the result. White oak is favored for exterior use.

Tree About 100 feet, sometimes up to 175 feet, high and 3 to 4 feet in diameter. Trunk columnar, quick growing.

Habitat Eastern North America.

Reuse Floors, cladding, decorative beams and mantels.

Surfaces Skip-planed: light to medium reddish-brown relief areas, circular-saw marks. Resurfaced: medium to coarse texture, subtle discolorations, knots can crack open and are often filled, nail holes.

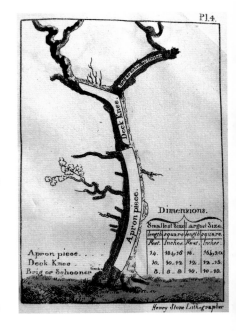

> Oak tree with cutting diagram for ship parts. Plate from *The Timber Merchant's Guide* by Peter Guillet, 1823.

> American oak, resurfaced
> *Quercus rubra, Quercus alba*

^
American oak, skip-planed
Quercus rubra, Quercus alba

>
White oak, resurfaced
Quercus alba

American Beech

Fagus grandifolia

Beech is a relatively common hardwood among the general mix of barnwoods. The joists and timbers vary in size and surface textures. As it is not a traditionally esteemed American hardwood, beech is easy to overlook. But under the rustic wide-plank surface, reclaimed beech picks up subtle streaks of brown and black color, stress cracks, oxidized nail holes, and, sometimes, long-dormant insect tracings, as well as other character marks.

We've seen a number of experienced woodworkers be struck by beech's unexpected character, especially after being oil-finished. But this is not the case with all reclaimed beech. Deep within a timber, the wood can have a more subdued character, closer to its state when new. Time in a barn can radically change all woods. But the transformation of beech is striking because it's unexpected. It can be skip-planed to retain some of the aged surface. It is sometimes combined with reclaimed barn maple and other hardwoods that are comparably light and close-grained.

Tree About
100 feet high
and 3 to 4 feet
in diameter,
with a straight
columnar trunk.
It has a smooth,
blue-gray bark.

Habitat Eastern
North America
with sugar maple,
birches, hemlock.

Reuse Floors,
cladding, picture
frames.

Surfaces
Resurfaced: light
brownish red,
fine texture,
hard, shades
of brown, nail
holes.

>
American beech,
skip-planed
Fagus grandifolia

Hickory

Carya species

Old reclaimed hickory isn't the most common barnwood—that would be oak—but it's the hardest, and it's generally found in the larger barn timbers. Hickory is so tough that General Andrew Jackson's soldiers nicknamed him after the wood, and the hard man went down in history as Old Hickory. Before advances in woodworking machinery made it economical to mill hickory for lumber, the trees were often cut down and abandoned, and the branches of the straight, shaggy-barked hickories that grow in the lowlands, or along riverbanks, were stripped of their sweet pecans. But the tough hardwood burned long and hot (think "hickory-smoked"), and it was ideal for the handles of tools and guns. In fact, the cool feel of hickory handles of all kinds was a part of life on the frontier. The wood was sought after for spokes on carriage wheels and for Windsor chairs.

There are dozens of hickory tree varieties, but, as barn timber, the wood likely comes from three species: shagbark, pignut, and bitternut hickory. They share uncommon hardness and density, weighing more than fifty pounds per cubic foot, making hard-wearing surfaces for floors and tabletops. But hickory's beauty makes it worthy of more visual applications, too—a headboard, cabinetry, or accent cladding. Its heartwood alternates in color between light cream and reddish-brown waves. The sharp cracks of the hardwood can oxidize into dark streaks that trail off like gun smoke. As with the other barn hardwoods, like elm, beech, and chestnut, the preference is often to reveal most or all of the bare figure and grain that distinguishes the wood.

Tree About 85 to 100 feet high and 3 to 4 feet in diameter. Trunk straight, columnar with a curious bark (shagbark) that peels off as gray plates resembling roof shingles, sometimes curling upward. The nuts are gathered in the wild for their tasty, aromatic kernels, and are sold commercially as hickory nuts.

Habitat Interior of eastern North America with box elder, green ash, cottonwood.

Reuse Floors, furniture.

Surfaces Resurfaced: pale brown with darker streaks, coarse texture, hard and heavy, sharp edges on checks.

^
President Andrew Jackson with his hickory cane. Print by Pendleton's Lithography, 1833.

>
Hickory, resurfaced
Carya species

American Elm

Ulmus americana

The elm tree ought to be commonplace, but not many of them exist today. Between the 1930s and the 1980s, Dutch elm disease—caused by a fungus spread by the elm bark beetle—killed off a majority of almost one hundred million American elms. The elm was once the tree of small-town America, growing up to 135 feet tall and arching into a high canopy. Charles Dickens, on a visit to New Haven, Connecticut, in 1842, wrote that the elms "bring about a kind of compromise between town and country; as each had met the other half-way, and shaken hands upon it." And the elm was "an old friend" not just on Main Street; it grew all over the nation. The elm is still with us, though examples are rare. There are great hopes for its revival, however, with researchers working to develop new, disease-resilient strains of

the tree. One of the largest surviving stands is in New York City's Central Park.

Blight and time have lent the hard, light brown figure of American elm rough charm and elegance. In reclaimed elm, as in the other barn hardwoods, small stress cracks, the occasional nail hole, insect tracings, knot disfigurations, and other features that don't exist in new wood, or are graded out, seem indispensable. The recovered elm can also be distinguished by translucent off-white and sepia streaks, reminiscent of old lace that's been stored for decades. A pale, haunting beauty characterizes the blighted surface. Reclaimed mills around the country produce elm flooring and cabinetry stock from the larger timbers, sometimes in a barnwood mix with other light close-grained hardwoods like beech, maple, and hickory.

Tree About 100 feet to 135 feet high and 6 to 10 feet in diameter. Trunk columnar until 35 to 70 feet, and growing upward to form a cup-shaped head.

Habitat Eastern North America with box elder, green ash, cottonwood.

Reuse Floors, furniture.

Surfaces Resurfaced: pale brown with reddish hue, medium coarse, insect tracings, checking.

^
The Central Park Mall, lined with American elm trees.

>
American elm, resurfaced
Ulmus americana

Eastern Hemlock

Tsuga canadensis

Eastern hemlock is a common softwood, often mixed with hardwoods in barns. Barn hemlock can range in size, from narrow siding to larger timbers. Traditionally seen as light, soft, and brittle, hemlock is nonetheless dense-grained and possesses a warm light brown tone. But it can be splintery in its rough-sawn stage, before fine millwork, and the brittleness can lead to the dislodging of loose knots. Its physical qualities also produce a uniquely textured and distressed surface that has made eastern hemlock a versatile reclaimed wood. There's also western hemlock, which is generally lighter in tone, and second-growth in quality. Nonetheless, it can develop rustic brown surfaces and is often grouped with the eastern variety.

Tree Up to 100 feet high and 2 to 3 feet in diameter. Gracefully branched. Flat needles, with the upper side dark green, whitish beneath.

Habitat Northeastern North America. Well-drained soils in association with red spruce and regional hardwoods.

Reuse Joists, floors, cladding, rustic furniture.

Surfaces Original, skip-planed, resurfaced.

^
Eastern hemlock, resurfaced
Tsuga canadensis

>
Eastern hemlock, original surface
Tsuga canadensis

Industrial Buildings

The bulk of the wood we reclaim comes from the vast number of warehouses, factories, and grain elevators originally constructed in the post–Civil War era through the early twentieth century—structures emblematic of the United States' rich industrial past. Their massive beams, joists, posts, and floorings are a repository of the nation's old-growth and second-growth coniferous forests, cut down to build a productive capitalist country. Luckily, in recent decades a movement to preserve some of these essential gems of American vernacular architectural history has arisen, and has worked to maintain or convert the structures of old factory towns like Lowell, Massachusetts, and Paterson, New Jersey.

When demolition or full gutting does occur, however, reclamation preserves the material culture represented by the tremendous amount of wood these buildings can yield. The beams, joists, posts, and flooring of a single factory might total one million board feet reclaimed, filling a hundred flatbed trucks.

The majority of that important material culture is made up of three towering conifers, spread across the nation: eastern white pine from the Northeast and the Great Lakes states, southern longleaf pine, and Douglas fir from the Pacific Northwest. In addition, we find just about any softwood that grew tall and straight enough to find a use as lumber, including spruce, fir, red pine, western hemlock, shortleaf, loblolly, and slash pine. Rock maple, often beautifully scarred and scratched by years of heavy use, is the one hardwood of note that is occasionally found in industrial buildings. Maple is often too difficult or costly to salvage, and so it is a rare treat when we can get our hands on it, as in the beautiful flooring from the Edison factory on page 94.

<
Demolition of an 1860s commercial warehouse at 351 Broadway, New York

>
Warehouse No. 11, Porter Screen Warehouse & Distributing Company, Winooski, Vermont, built 1901, closed 1952.

<
Warehouse, New Bedford, Massachusetts, built before 1850. Today, the building houses a restaurant.

^
Water Works Park, Paterson, New Jersey. Detroit Publishing Company, c. 1900–06. Once silk factories, these buildings are now in ruins.

>
Cloth Room-Section 15, Massachusetts Mills, Lowell, Massachusetts. Founded at this location in 1839, the mills expanded for almost a century, closing in 1928. Some of these former mills are now apartment buildings.

White Pine

Pinus strobus

White pine is the oldest industrial wood, and the most widely used from colonial times to the second half of the nineteenth century. Colonial life was ensconced in white pine, which was used for paneling, floors, furniture, clapboard siding, and even soup bowls (called treenware). Pine floors were especially revered. Scrubbed, shellacked, and waxed, trodden day after day, and mellowed by the sun, they picked up an ethereal amber tone that earned the wood the name pumpkin pine (it was earlier known as apple pine).

Reclaimed from industrial structures, white pine is found in both joists and larger timbers. It was harvested early on in the Northeast, and later in the Great Lakes regions of Michigan, Wisconsin, and Minnesota. Reclaimed white pine is seen in all surface options. The original aged surface has a soft, feathered texture and a patina of warm rustic brown tones. Skip-planing brings into relief some of the bare light-toned wood grain and figure. If boards are resurfaced, the soft, light tan wood has an even grain and figure, with knots and occasional nail holes and stress cracks.

Tree About 190 to 330 feet high and 3 to 6 feet in diameter. Bluish-green needles in groups of five, and long, narrow pendant cones. Of great vitality, quick-growing, and durable. Rapidly recolonizes abandoned agricultural lands.

Habitat Northeastern North America west to the Great Lakes states. Well-drained soils, often forming homogeneous woods.

Reuse Floors, cladding, cabinetry, furniture.

Surfaces Original: light to medium browns, feathered texture, up-down saw or circular-saw marks. Skip-planed: gradual tonal transition between aged and relief areas, pronounced saw marks and impacts. Resurfaced: tan to pale red brown, subtle and even grain, varied knot size, old knots loose at edges.

^
Pine joists awaiting removal during demolition of the Edgar Laing stores in Lower Manhattan. Photograph by Jack E. Boucher, 1971. The five cast-iron-front buildings were erected by architect and inventor James Bogardus in 1849.

>
White pine, skip-planed
Pinus strobus

^
Bedroom with pine floor,
Van Cortlandt House
Museum, The Bronx, built
beginning in 1748.

>
White pine, resurfaced
Pinus strobus

Longleaf Pine

Pinus palustris

In the late nineteenth century, the longleaf pine forests generated a ready supply of structural wood for industry and also for bridges, railroad carriages and sleepers, and fencing; it was used to make charcoal, too. But lumber wasn't the first commodity to be exploited in high volume from the tree. It was, instead, the pine sap, extracted through deep cuts into the tree's outer layer. Products created from the thick, tacky liquid were called "naval stores," encompassing everything from water sealers for wooden ships to paint, varnish, and shoe polish. The tree wasn't used just to build ships; it was a commodity on board.

Longleaf was so common and so valued in the late nineteenth century that it is regularly salvaged from a broad range of industrial structures, including mills, factories, warehouses, horse stables, and stores. Among the smaller-size lumber is decking approximately three to four inches thick, joined by splines. This is supported by three- or four-inch-thick joists. Larger timbers frame the structure.

Longleaf is nearly as hard as oak. In 1892, the Society of Chemical Industry in Great Britain extended the highest accolades to longleaf: "The long-leaf pine is known to be superior to all the other species in strength and durability. In tensile strength, it is said to approach, and perhaps surpass, cast iron. In cross-breaking strength it rivals the oak, requiring, it is stated, 10,000 lb. pressure per square inch to break it. In stiffness, it is superior to oak by from 50–100 per cent."

The wood of reclaimed longleaf is light red to orange, with a marked contrast of light and dark across the growth rings. The growth rings are often dense, and it is not uncommon to see as many as twenty-five seasonal rings per inch. In its original reclaimed state, longleaf has an aged brown surface and characteristic warm tones. Each alteration— from brushed dirty top to spot-sanded, to skip-planed, to fully planed and smooth— produces a different look and feel. Resurfaced, it's further graded and refined into knotty, select (some knots and flat-sawn wood), and clear vertical grain pine, traditionally called "comb grade" here in the Northeast, where it was a row house standard. There is typically iron nail bleed and surface checking, and, often, limited but sound knot content.

Tree About 100 to 130 feet high and 2 to 3 feet in diameter. Trunk tall, straight, and with few branches. Bark pale orange-brown. Deep-rooted.

Habitat Belt along the Atlantic and Gulf Coasts in southeastern North America.

Reuse Floors, paneling, millwork, timbers, furniture.

Surfaces Original: medium to deep brown, circular-saw marks, occasional face nails. Skip-planed: deep amber relief areas, pronounced saw marks. Resurfaced: reddish orange, straight and uneven grain, occasional nail holes.

^
Longleaf pine joists stacked at a demolition site in New York City.

>
Longleaf pine, comb grade
Pinus palustris

^
Southern pine, original surface
Pinus palustris

>
Longleaf pine, select grade
Pinus palustris

Sinker Pine

Pinus palustris

Sinker woods are logs that sank to the bottom of rivers or lakes during the log drives of the 1800s and early 1900s. Deadheads is another term for them. Either way, cool water, low oxygen levels, and tree resin combine to create a natural preservation process. Submerged a century or longer, the logs absorb minerals from the water that infuse soft, mineralized hues at this early stage of petrification. Most sinker logs are longleaf pine or cypress, but we have seen white pine and, in one instance, chestnut (page 58). Many millions of logs no doubt remain in waters across the country, like sunken old-growth treasure. The harvesting operations happen in rivers and lakes wherever records of old log drives indicate possible finds.

A sinker log will have the same rich color and grain density as one that successfully reached the mill. They just parted ways on the river a long time ago—one floated off to American civilization, and the other sank, though it was really just delayed en route. So we include sinker woods as a reclaimed resource, as they still carry old-growth beauty, history, and sustainability. But the look is distinct. Sinker doesn't have the nail holes, stress cracks, and colorations that you see in industrial reclaimed wood. Sinker logs are milled into flooring, paneling, and lumber for mantels and furniture.

^
Log drivers at work on the swift Diamond River in northern New Hampshire. Photograph by Victor Beaudoin, c. 1930s.

>
Longleaf pine, sinker grade
Pinus palustris

Douglas Fir

Pseudotsuga menziesii

Not a fir but a close relative of hemlock, Douglas fir grew nearly as tall as many redwoods in the mountainous virgin stands of the West Coast, where the misty air links land and sea and turns trees into skyscrapers. From the Pacific Coast, the tree's range extends eastward to milder climates beyond the Cascade Mountains and into the Rockies, where it mixes with hemlock, Sitka spruce, and sugar pine; and northward to pure stands in Oregon above the Umpqua River. For centuries, the Native Americans of the region utilized the tree, along with the massive cedar, for buildings, totem poles, and everyday items. In the United States, it has long been a staple of the building trade, and favored for railroad sleepers, posts, and firewood. Exported to Europe, it has become a popular woodland and park tree. Today, the old-growth forests of Douglas fir have become a modern battleground between government and industry, as they are home to the endangered spotted owl.

Douglas fir, the product of the massive old-growth tree, is reclaimed from commercial warehouses and factories across the country, pilings in the Great Lakes and Hudson River regions, dismantled bridges, army bases, storage tanks (page 127), and other sources. Its versatile properties and beauty have made it an all-purpose wood in old-growth, second-growth, and, increasingly, plantation-grown varieties. The wood is hard enough to be viable as flooring and is ideal for wall paneling. Given its warm tones, clear figure, and stability, it was popular with mid-century modern designers. It can also be highly figured and exhibit curly spirals that are wild and gamy, as if the wood in the tree is high on the mushrooms that grow in the old-growth soil where the tree is rooted.

Reclaimed Douglas fir has been a test case for the viability of grading salvaged wood. The matter was pursued by Robert H. Falk of the USDA Forest Services Laboratory in Madison, Wisconsin, in the 1990s. Falk's conclusion was cautious but hopeful: "I like to say that the reclaimed wood is nicer, it's richer, it has more growth rings. But is it stronger after all those years? The study of Douglas Fir led us to conclude that it depends. You can't say with certainty. You can have bolt holes, notches, splits and a variety of things. And that's the kicker. You don't know, because every piece is different. At the cellular level, the wood may be stronger. At the macro level, it may not be stronger. But it doesn't matter if A is stronger than B, if both A and B are strong enough."

Tree About 200 to
230 feet high and
3 to 4 feet in
diameter, but up
to 13 and 15 feet
in diameter.

Habitat Pacific
Northwest, forms
mountain forests
by itself.

Reuse Floors,
paneling,
millwork,
timbers,
furniture.

Surfaces
Original: aged
light to deep
browns, circular-
saw marks.
Skip-planed:
light to reddish-
brown relief
areas, sound.
Resurfaced:
beige to reddish
brown, medium
and relatively
uniform texture,
but can have wild
and curly grain.

^
Douglas fir columns and stringers, Harmon mattress factory, Tacoma, Washington, built in the early twentieth century.

>
Douglas fir, resurfaced
Pseudotsuga menziesii

Maple

Acer saccharum

Maple's clear, close-grain surface, cream-toned hue, and ability to take a stain made it a favorite for furniture and specialty uses, but in the nineteenth century, it was likely to be overlooked by the lumbermen as yielding tough, narrow boards. Over time it found its limited place in factory construction, thanks to its extreme durability. This wood can take a beating, and given a hundred years, machinery and steel wheels make deep impressions in maple factory floors. As reclaimed wood, when you can find it, it definitely has character. If it's to your taste, take it exactly as you find it, as in this sample from a demolished 1895 Edison factory's floor in Bloomfield, New Jersey.

When woodworking equipment improved, maple found a new use in gym floors and bowling alleys (page 118).

Tree About 100 feet high or more and 3 to 5 feet in diameter. Known for its spectacular fall foliage and as a source of maple syrup. It can live up to four hundred years, with the capability of "hydraulic lift," drawing water from lower soil levels into dry areas that aid the tree and all the plants growing around it.

Habitat Well drained soils in eastern North America, and in network with beech, birch, hemlock, and black cherry. Sometimes forming woods on its own.

Reuse Floors, furniture, paneling.

Surfaces Often preserved with original marks. Otherwise belt-sanded or skip-planed and then film coated.

>
Factory maple, original surface
Acer saccharum

Wooden Tanks

Wooden tanks are a relatively low volume source of reclaimed wood of exceptional quality. The woods are found in large—sometimes massive—wooden vessels that store liquids. We've seen tanks used for wine, vinegar, brandy, vermouth, pickles, whiskey, beer, water, and Worcestershire sauce. And there are cooling tanks, used to store water for industrial applications. There is no typical geographical distribution—they can be found in the American heartland and on New York City roofs.

The species of woods do fall within a limited range. They're known for their performance in resisting water and rot, and they're stable, easy to work, and free from knots. Tank woods often come from old-growth trees, in a grade that a luthier might use for a stringed instrument. The species include redwood, bald cypress, cedar, and oak, which are standard at many liquor distilleries. We've also come across Douglas fir, considered ideal for Worcestershire sauce tanks (page 127).

Modern tanks are large-scale versions of the historical ones, up to twenty feet high and as wide across. There's not much keeping the thick bevel staves (often two inches or more thick) together besides pressure and some steel tension bands at intervals—as it's been done for centuries.

Reclaimed tank woods do not face some of the challenges of other wood salvage. They practically dismantle themselves, being joined on their edges with simple wood dowels. They're taken down after their useful life, which can vary greatly by use and species, or in the course of a larger demolition project. Long before that time, they've picked up their characteristic exterior wear. The quality of the wood grain can echo that of an ancient tree, making us regret that the wood was ever taken in the first place. But there is sometimes no substitute in maintaining the standards of certain beverages, and the relative volume of lumber that is needed is low.

<
Wood over Manhattan: The Starrett-Lehigh Building, built 1931. Alaskan yellow cedar or, rarely, cypress and redwood are used for the iconic water tanks.

>
Oak from distillery staves. Note the slight curve and bevel made to form the round tank.

Bald Cypress

Taxodium distichum

The extreme rot- and insect-resistance of cypress is the product of long evolution in the southeastern swamps. The heartwood contains high concentrations of cypressene oil, a natural preservative the color of golden honey. The tree itself is strong and elegant, with soft leaves and small, dark cones. It grows slowly in the swamps and tidewaters and can live for more than one thousand years. The tree has an unusual form, with thick wood stems, called cypress knees, projecting out from the roots.

Historically, bald cypress was made into shingles that wore like slate and watertight ships' hulls and caskets. The last evokes the reason settlers often wanted to clear the cypress swamps, which they considered to be filled with mosquito-borne disease and deadly snakes and alligators.

Reclaimed cypress is sourced from wooden vinegar and water tanks, and, like other tank woods, is a highly refined grade of clear, dense heartwood. It's rich with natural oils and has exceptional exterior performance, but the beauty of its grain and figure makes it desirable for interior applications like paneling and cabinetry. It was favored by Frank Lloyd Wright, who saw wood as, "the most humanly intimate of all materials." The cathedral forms of old-growth cypress's flat-sawn figure creates striking patterns, with tones made richer by the density of the growth rings. The exterior side of a tank board develops mint-gray and whitewashed hues, and shows the characteristic marks of steel bands. Cypress is most widely used in the American South, often together with longleaf pine, where both are deeply tied to local history and culture. But the beauty and rarity of cypress lends it universal appeal.

```
Tree About
165 feet high
and 8 to 10 feet
in diameter.
Trunk has
large root
buttresses and
often develops
knee-like bumps
from the roots,
especially when
growing in water.
Short shoots
with their
needles are shed
entire, hence
the tree's
alternate name
bald cypress.

Habitat Forms
woods in swamps,
in open water,
or in association
with other
wetland trees
of southeastern
North America.
```

```
Reuse Paneling,
cabinetry,
millwork.

Surfaces
Original:
light green
to mint-green
colorations,
darkened recessed
band marks,
fine leathery
texture.
Resurfaced:
yellow brown,
exceptionally
dense grain,
clear, fine
grain.
```

>
Bald cypress, resurfaced
Taxodium distichum

<
Scene in the cypress swamp along the Natchez Trace Parkway, Canton, Mississippi. Photograph by Carol M. Highsmith.
Note the cypress knees.

>
Bald cypress, original surface
Taxodium distichum

>
Bald cypress, resurfaced comb grade
Taxodium distichum

Redwood

Sequoia sempervirens

Running along a narrow range in California and southern Oregon, and set back from the Pacific Coast, redwood forests are pure stands, with the oldest living trees dating from more than two thousand years ago. They are descendants of trees that witnessed the dinosaurs and once covered a far greater area across North America: Just 5 percent of the original forests that predate European settlement remain. Imagine having twenty times the redwood forests that we now have.

The tallest tree on the planet, a mature redwood's roots intertwine with the roots of surrounding trees to anchor it. It hosts a city of insects and plants and moves thirty-seven thousand tons of water a day. Centuries of life in the redwood tree produce wood of depth and beauty. "The redwoods," wrote John Steinbeck (*Travels with Charley: In Search of America*) in 1962, "once seen, leave a mark.... From them comes silence and awe ... they are not like any trees we know, they are ambassadors from another time."

Redwood is salvaged from cooling tanks and sometimes from wine or vinegar casks—and the rare Fifth Avenue water tank. The wood has remarkable resistance to moisture and rot. It's light, soft, easy to work, and stable. And clear and knot-free boards are more the rule than the exception. All these qualities account for the wood's renowned beauty as well as its exterior performance. The aged surface of reclaimed redwood is a noble red or red brown. The density of the old-growth grain can be so fine that it appears to trail off without end. The Native Americans thought the tree would live forever; when we reclaim redwood, that may be true. Straight- or wavy-figured, reclaimed redwood can pick up dark mineral streaks. And, during the wood's life of liquid storage, its exterior can turn smooth and leather-like. The aged face is also impressed at intervals with dark band marks from iron hoops that secured the wooden tank staves. Both the aged and resurfaced sides of tank boards are used in design, often for wall paneling or as furniture and tabletops.

<u>Tree</u> About 200 to 330 feet high, with some said to reach 400 feet high, and up to 16 feet in diameter. Bark 5 to 10 inches thick. Resprouts vigorously from dormant buds following forest fires.

<u>Habitat</u> Coastal mountain ranges of California and southern Oregon. Forms homogeneous woods on damp sandstone.

<u>Reuse</u> Paneling, exterior.

<u>Surfaces</u> Original: dark reddish browns, darker recessed ferrous lines, aged leathery texture. Resurfaced: deep reddish brown, tight grain, clear and soft, straight or pronounced flat-sawn figure.

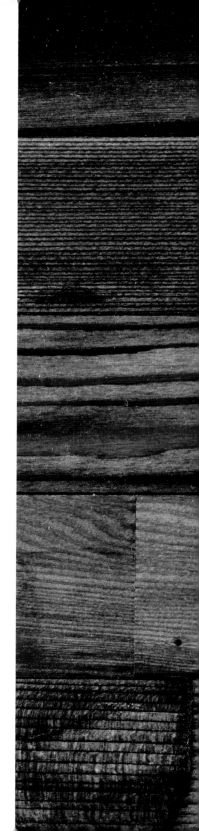

>
California redwood, resurfaced with oil finish
Sequoia sempervirens

^
California redwood,
original surface
Sequoia sempervirens

>
*Section of the Grizzly Giant, 101
feet circumference.* Photograph
by Carleton E. Watkins, Mariposa
Grove, Yosemite, 1865–66.

Alaskan Yellow Cedar

Cupressus nootkatensis

A handful of tree species in the *Cupressaceae* family produce cedarwood—some are rare and protected in American wildlife refuges and wetlands, like the Great Dismal Swamp in Virginia and North Carolina and the Apalachicola National Forest in Florida. Cedar trees are bare of branches for most of their ash-gray trunks, and their small purplish cones are berry-like, in stark contrast to the cones of other conifers. They're uniquely adapted to swampy environments, where the trees grow slow and strong (some for up to nine hundred years), acquiring natural resistance to moisture and insects.

The early settlers may have gained appreciation for cedar from Native Americans, and, for a long time, it was the main wood for exterior use, especially for shingles, in the eastern United States. Splitting shingles was once common labor. In the twentieth century, cedar retreated to backyard structures, utility poles, and tanks. Alaskan yellow cedar, an especially desirable species, will likely fill the New York City skyline in the form of water tanks for a long time to come. Given the wood's limited applications and our tendency to use it until it rots, there is not a lot of reclaimed cedar, nor is there high demand for it, as new cedar is relatively low in cost and available. The value of reclaimed tank cedar is generally in its aesthetic appeal—commonly, in its weathered exterior face, with its grayed surface and irregular pattern of band marks.

Tree About 165 feet high and 7 to 8 feet in diameter. Trunk tall and straight. Bark cinnamon red, with a dense covering of scales. Inner chamber of seed coat with red liquid balsamic resin.

Habitat All soil types in western North America into Alaska; high ground as well as water meadows

Reuse Paneling, exterior.

Surfaces Original: weathered-gray tones, ferrous lines from metal bands. Grain unusually dense.

> ^
> A modern cedar water tank, New York City.

> >
> Alaskan yellow cedar, original surface
> *Cupressus nootkatensis*

Curious and Uncommon

The rubric "curious and uncommon" covers woods we haven't yet discussed—though only those that fall within this book's defined scope, since reclaimed wood eludes comprehensiveness. We're drawn to rarities, like those that filled the cabinets of curiosity that were popular among kings, merchants, and scientists in Europe in the 1600s. The cabinets' contents were microcosms of the world's wonders and natural history. The finds of wood salvage are far more modest but still unique, and always pure Americana.

The sources here are a mixed lot, and generalizations are hard to make. They are largely woods that were harvested in recent eras, dating from the mid-twentieth century.

Some of these sources are, or were, common: bowling alleys and gym courts, for instance. Value can also be found in high turnover crating, like cargo cherry—a massive trove, but hard to extract. Other sources, like mushroom wood, are the result of natural processes. And still others, seem like an old lumber sideshow that P. T. Barnum might have trumpeted: strange and exotic, like General Tom Thumb or the Fiji Mermaid.

<
Southeast Asian tropical hardwoods sourced from Japanese cargo ship crating.

v
Atlantic City boardwalk. Photograph by Arthur Nager, 1972.

Boardwalks

Miles of late twentieth-century boardwalks along the East Coast have been dismantled or upended by storms. Many were made of extraordinary hardwoods from the South American rain forests with seemingly supernatural resistance to moisture and insects, replacing the old-growth Douglas fir from their previous incarnations. The narrow tropical surface boards, smoothed by weather and foot traffic, sometimes offer up an intricate pattern of micro-checks in gray tones that resembles a satellite view of the Amazon. The species, which are often grouped together as ipê but also include cumaru, angélique, greenheart, and an odd stick of purpleheart, are varied in color and fine-grained. The boardwalks' substructures, of larger dimensions, can also be tropical species.

For all that these sometime fabled walkways represent to people, their tropical boards are emblematic of rain-forest loss. The damage, relative to the loss of Northern Hemisphere hardwoods, is exponential, as larger swaths of the jungle are felled to access commercial logs. The impact on diversity is, of course, well documented. It's hard to say whether boardwalks are the only sustainable source of rain-forest woods, but they're a rare pleasure.

^
Atlantic City boardwalk,
resurfaced
Dicorynia guianensis,
Tabebuia species,
Dipteryx odorata

>
Coney Island boardwalk,
original surface
Dicorynia guianensis,
Tabebuia species,
Dipteryx odorata

Mushroom Wood

Mushroom wood is made not of mushrooms but of eastern hemlock. And although it looks primeval, it's often from a relatively young tree. Its texture is a direct result of its use in mushroom farming. At growing facilities, where the hemlock boards frame earth-filled mushroom beds, mushrooms penetrate the young softwood fibers to extract nutrients—a reflection of the symbiotic exchange between trees and mushrooms, which spring from sprawling mycorrhizal networks below ground.

The boards are generally in eight-inch widths. Because of its extreme texture, mushroom wood is most often used as decorative paneling. Typically, we brush the boards mechanically to remove dirt, which allows the wood to retain its rich earthy browns. Edges are then ripped square and the boards are back planed.

>
Mushroom wood
Tsuga canadensis

Cargo Woods

The lumber crating required for shipping heavy goods often gets scrapped. We come across so-called cargo oak (both red and white), cherry, hickory, and a remarkable variety of Southeast Asian tropical hardwoods that are large enough to resaw. They are not old-growth woods, nor were they long used, but they have saw marks and enough aged appeal to fit into the mainstream of reclaimed antique and vintage woods. They are most commonly remilled for flooring or paneling, or the original stock is used for tabletops.

Japanese Cargo Overseas cargo woods are stamped to identify Japan as their place of origin (page 108), but the trees, we found, grew in tropical forests. The species were a mystery until lab identification revealed they came from Southeast Asia (Indonesia, Myanmar, and the Philippines) and included thitka (*Pentace malvaceae*), coralwood (*Adenanthera mimosoideae*), and limpato (*Prainea moraceae*). Two and a half by three inches in the rough, they are aged to deep browns, blacks, and grays, with broad stripe patterns from the impressions of metal bands. Like other reclaimed woods, they have rustic and refined design options. They are often ripped to narrow thickness for decorative paneling and interior use. Exterior furniture applications at thicker dimensions capitalize on their exotic look and durable nature.

American Cargo These domestic second-growth hardwoods, commonly cherry and oak are two by six inches, rough-sawn, and gray- or brown-toned. Cargo cherry has the same aged texture as cargo oak, but is closer in color to a reddish burnt sienna. Similar-type stock includes horse-farm fencing from Kentucky and corral boards, as they're called in the Rocky Mountain region.

∧
Elephants haul logs from the Taungoo forest in Myanmar, a stronghold of biodiversity under threat. Some hardwood cargo-ship crating may be the byproduct of illegal teak logging in areas like this. In Myanmar, for example, confiscated hardwood logs are often auctioned by the government.

>
Japanese cargo, original surface
Pentace malvaceae, Adenanthera mimosoideae, Prainea moraceae

^
American cargo oak,
original surface
Quercus rubra, Quercus alba

>
American cargo cherry,
resurfaced
Prunus serotina

Gyms and Bowling Alleys

It wasn't until woodworking equipment improved, tastes changed, and American indoor sports took off that maple became popular for gym floors, basketball courts, bowling alleys, roller rinks, and racquetball courts. These are sources of cleaner maple for reclamation than factory flooring, although in the case of gym floors, the boards can be extremely narrow and may not amount to much after remilling.

When bowling alleys are closed, as they have often been in recent decades, and the shoes, bowling balls, and pins have been handed off to friends or sold on eBay, the wooden lanes are often salvaged. Made of rock maple that often transitions to heart pine, they still have a lot of life. Given the lanes' butcher-block assembly— the wood is about two inches thick and intersected by steel rods at close intervals—they're challenging to salvage and remanufacture. They require care and multiple blades to saw into custom dimensions. The alleys are also coated with about the hardest industrial-strength clear-coat finish that exists. It doesn't mean that these woods are not worth the effort. The refined wood grains, the butcher-block aesthetic, and the long history of sports and bowling in the United States give these woods great appeal.

^^
Bowling alleys, Paul Smith's Hotel, Adirondack Mountains, New York. Detroit Publishing Company, 1900–1905.

^
YMCA gymnasium. National Photo Company, c. 1910. Note the elevated wooden running track around the perimeter of the room.

>
Bowling alley
Acer saccharum, Pinus palustris

<
Racquetball court
Acer saccharum

>
Gym floor
Acer saccharum

>
Running track
Picea rubens
Note marks left by
spiked running shoes

Pilings and Docks

Wood pilings or docks are outlier sources. We've salvaged them from the Hudson River, and they are occasionally sourced from the Great Lakes region. They're generally a mid-range grade of Douglas fir or pine from the 1950s, but they are perfectly preserved, revealing translucent mineral tones when sawed open.

The round pilings are unique as a reclaimed wood in their capacity as thin veneer applications for paneling and cabinetry. Otherwise, they are resawn like other logs. Decorative flooring, paneling, and furniture are their main applications.

^
Lusitania *docking at new Hudson River piers.* Bain News Service, November 20, 1908. Pier 56, at Fourteenth Street, is now a field of pilings in the water waiting to be reclaimed.

>
Docks and pilings, resurfaced *Pinus echinata, Pseudotsuga menziesii*

Reclaimed millwork generates significant amounts of rejected wood—its waste factor, aside from sawdust: so-called "aged skins," naily edges, or crosscut ends. The daily tempest of scrap typically gets turned into mulch or fuel or waste. But this heavily distressed mix can also be freed up and reclaimed. The panels in this series represent a range of small lots. Boardwalk edges, whale-oiled timber, naily barnwood, curly grain Douglas fir: each escaped the scrap pile, with striking results. Reclaimed cypress lumber that contains holes left by a fungus that destroys the heart of the tree, called pecky cypress (pages 44–45), while not to everyone's taste, commands a premium.

^
Scraps and oddities of historical woods ramble to the edge of the lumberyard.

>
Northeast softwood, naily edges (trim waste) Generations of nail types may be found in a single board

<
Douglas fir, resurfaced
with oil finish
Pseudotsuga menziesii
Source: Worcestershire
sauce tank

>
Boardwalk edges
Dicorynia guianensis,
Tabebuia species,
Dipteryx odorata

>
Whale-oil pine, resurfaced
Pinus palustris
Source: Plymouth Cordage
Company, Massachusetts,
c. 1830

CHAPTER

4

RECLAMATION

Demolition

It's hard to imagine the virgin forests stored within old buildings—until they reemerge as pieces of lumber, after a century or more, through the demolition process. Salvaged, as they are, with heavy nail patterns, aged and stress-cracked, and sometimes scorched by fire, they appear degraded at a job site. In high-density urban zones, old buildings still go down the way they went up: largely by hand—with the sledgehammers, pickaxes, and shovels. Outside cities, machinery is set loose, including the Terex excavator, with the jaws of a T-rex, which replaced the wrecking ball, and the Bobcat, a little tank with claws.

Years ago, demolition companies were proud to be called house wreckers. Today, an added measure of care is taken with the old lumber. The regard is tied to the newly recognized value of the wood, and to the requirements of modern extraction strategies and safety guidelines, as seen in the photograph of the crosscutting of a joist end and its lowering by rope (page 230). Barn removal is a very different process and culture, as mentioned earlier. Time and space, and the strictures at urban sites, don't appear to be issues.

What wood gets salvaged is determined by a range of factors—its physical qualities; the presence of contaminants like paint, metal, and wood rot; and, mostly, its size. We look primarily for lumber that is 3 x 8 inches x 8 feet or larger—wood that can be resawn to yield wide planks. Smaller dimensions are acceptable in barn siding, industrial flooring, and other sources where the prized patina and limited nail content make it viable to process and reuse the wood. But each project proceeds case by case. The incentives of generating value and saving disposal costs go a long way toward justifying reclamation, even if taking down the heavy timbers "requires back-breaking strength, like dismantling the pyramids," says Chris Garafolo, site manager at 351 Broadway, where we photographed the demolition seen in this chapter. You can still come across wreckers who are already sold on the idea and "hate to see the stuff thrown away." They may have wood shops where they build on weekends.

> Whether it's good or bad, it is sometimes very pleasant, too, to smash things.
>
> —Fyodor Dostoyevsky, *Notes from Underground* (1864)

<<
Barnwood: hickory, wormy maple, beech, maple.

< >
Reclaimed lumber waits at 351 Broadway during demolition.

Lumberyard and Millworks

A reclaimed-lumber mill isn't a conventional sawmill, though it has the same modern equipment. The mills are as different as the old-growth forest and modern tree farms that supply their inventories. We've seen reclaimed yards and mills located in all kinds of places—in the backwoods and in new construction along a highway, on the outskirts of cities and in former barns or warehouses.

The yard is often managed by a crew who handle the inventory of bundled lumber and big timber, often in tight spaces. Cesar Garcia and Brian Hurley, who run our yards, move from manual work to forklift operation throughout the day. Raw material is retrieved for processing, flatbeds pull up for unloading, the yard is always a work in progress. You never step in the same yard twice. Reclaimed woods, with their irregular sizes, rarely stack flat, presenting a hazard, no matter the weather. An inventory system can often be a challenge, and is more likely to be stored in an owner's head than in a computer.

The revival of old woods starts with the removal of nails, of layers of dirt and dust, and maybe of paint. Even when cleared of bits of metal, the lumber is heavier than new and can have thick resins that gum up machines. The noise of the sawmill fills the air, but, when it's down, the space echoes with hammers tapping, squeaking pry bars, and the forklift engine. For us, it's an industrial version of the wildlife sounds in the Connecticut Valley outside.

It's only when the resawn and dried lumber arrives at the fine millwork stage that the transformed material reaches modern times. The space is clean, and the machines, though loud, have a quieter buzz and hum than the sawmill. The machine blades, however, are still wary of aged surfaces and dense grains, and of the blade-destroying nail. In the end, about 50 percent or less of the original raw material leaves as finished reclaimed product. The waste is burned for fuel or turned to landscape mulch.

I came to see the buildings as fossils of time past. . . . The men were all dead, but the buildings were still here, left behind as the city grew around them. . . . The passing of buildings was for me a great event.

—Danny Lyon, *The Destruction of Lower Manhattan* (1966)

<
Demolition in progress,
351 Broadway.

^
Cool dry storage, Armster
Reclaimed Lumber Co.,
Springfield, Massachusetts.

>>
The portable sawmill cuts wood
into dimensional lumber.

Remanufacturing Reclaimed Wood: The Ten-Step Process

1

Inventory Storage
Reclaimed lumber
is transported,
sometimes over
thousands of
miles, to the
mill on long
flatbed trucks,
unloaded,
tallied, and
stacked in
covered or
exposed storage.

2

De-nailing
Nails and other
metal are removed
as detailed
on page 140.
The process is
time- and labor-
intensive, but
vital. The woods
are then ready
to be received by
the sawyers and
fine millworkers.

3

Resawing
Boards are sawn
into "blanks";
often 4/4 (1-
inch thick) for
flooring and
paneling. Blade
changes forced by
soot, dust, and
heavy resins are
frequent. Every
board and timber
requires care and
focus to be sawn
for optimal yield
and requested
grade.

4

Grading
Cracked, warped,
narrow, or
rotted material
is removed.
Each board face
is carefully
inspected.

5

Kiln-drying
Antique wood
is often said
to be dry and
stable, but
kiln-drying is
often a critical
step. The kiln's
temperature, air
circulation, and
humidity levels
work to release
water from the
wood to under 10
percent moisture
content.

6

Ripping
The rough edges
are ripped on one
or both sides to
produce square
boards.

7

Planing
One or both faces
is "dressed" by
the roughing
planer. The
salvaged woods
continue to be
abusive to the
equipment down
the line and
force painstaking
blade changes.
The faces of the
boards are planed
smooth, skip-
planed, or left
in the rough,
based on orders.

8

Molding
This precision-
millwork stage
typically adds
a tongue and
groove, shiplap,
clapboard, or
other profile.

9

End trimming
The boards are
trimmed square
on the ends or
end-matched for
installation.

10

Shipment
The extra long
and irregular
lengths of
reclaimed
wood are often
transported by
a company truck
or packaged for
common carrier.

>
clockwise from top
Resawing mill, planing mill,
ripping a plank.

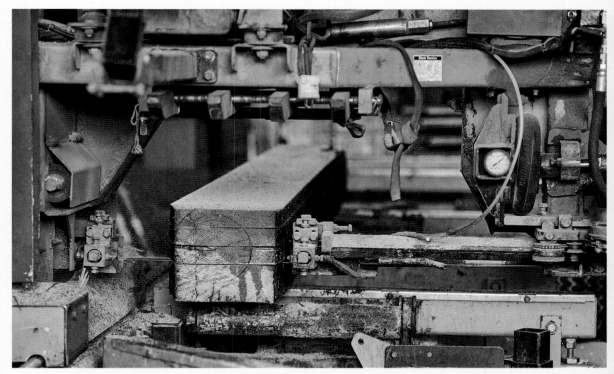

Doing It Yourself

Reclaimed wood can be a challenge to source, and equally difficult to prepare and work. However, we support the do-it-yourselfer. From our perspective, there's a great return in having a direct hand in the wood's transformation and revival and in living with wood you've reclaimed. To us, it's like alchemy, the ancient practice of trying to turn base metals into gold. In alchemical terms, salvaged wood is *prima materia,* or unformed, unsuspecting, and degraded raw material.

The following notes, based on our experience, primarily focus on finding and preparing the salvaged woods to be worked. We have not provided instructions for woodworking projects and techniques. There are vast resources available in print and online.

If you're planning on salvaging wood yourself, sources that come readily to mind are local reuse centers, online listings, and demolition sites. What turns up can be hit-or-miss. And there are other obstacles. Demo sites can be intimidating to approach—and a hazard. There may be issues of transport and getting wood cut to manageable size. There may even be shame, in the case of rummaging through dumpsters or curbside, though it's hard to find fault with salvaging material. In the case of centuries-old wood, it's all diamonds in the rough. People looking to work with reclaimed wood often develop an eye for spotting it and for scouting out the resource.

The easiest way to acquire reclaimed wood is to visit mills and reuse centers that remill the woods. Many welcome walk-ins, and, though they're not likely to be nearby if you live in an urban area, they can all offer a memorable experience. They may require a long road trip to get to, not unlike rural destinations for lower-cost antiques. At Sawkill Lumber, we established a warehouse space in Brooklyn to make semi-milled reclaimed material more readily available. Local sourcing offers obvious benefits of quality control, lower delivery costs, and higher sustainability. And there's what some have termed "locaphilia," or the connection to local history (modeled on E. O. Wilson's concept of biophilia, or our connection to nature).

The larger reclaimed mills, however, generally serve the trade, so what's available may depend on what's in progress. The reclaimed lumber in stock can be at various stages of the process, from in-the-rough to fully milled paneling. There may be overruns on orders, or returned lots, or woods that were graded out. "Skins," or aged surfaces trimmed from a timber, may be for sale. These extremely distressed surfaces can have extraordinary character. The same is true for odd pieces of timber with unusual joinery ends. Or lots with sublime patina. There can be rare species like reclaimed red gum or sassafras that may not be on a website. Much of this material has also cleared some critical hurdles—being dry, metal free, and sawn to a workable size. Prices may be discounted but are still higher than a new lumber outlet's prices. Relative to other salvage options listed above, however, there are the advantages of reduced waste, saved time, and expanded choice.

If you are considering reclaimed woods for a project, don't be afraid to ask questions. A good mill will educate and inform you, engaging your interest and trust. As no industry grading standards for reclaimed wood exist, your instincts as a buyer are key. Here are a few basic things you'll want to know if you're contemplating a project using reclaimed wood:

Are samples and photos available? Do they represent current stock? What further variations may be expected? As you'll see in the design chapter of this book, some projects emphasize the tonal and textural variations in reclaimed wood, while others seek a consistent look and feel. How much variation you can live with is dependent on your project.

How is the grade described? What is the heartwood and sapwood content? What is the overall grain density, as described in growth rings per inch? What is the prevalence of nail holes? Generally, higher grades, no matter what the mill's nomenclature, will have denser grain structure and fewer knots and holes.

What is the estimated waste factor, that is, the additional amount of wood you'll need to purchase to complete your project? This relates to open knots, end splits, heavy checks, tonal variations, and so forth. A good average for reclaimed wood is 15 percent, including trim waste.

What is the available range of sizes, both widths and lengths, for the wood you want? Wider and longer is always more costly, but both are essential design considerations for any project.

How is moisture content handled? Is the wood kiln dried or air dried? To avoid unwelcome wood movement after installation, kiln-dried wood is generally preferable for most applications.

Preparation

If you're buying wood that hasn't been processed by a professional, you'll need to prepare it for woodworking. Here's an overview of the steps involved in the process.

Get to know the wood

Assess the size, condition, and nail content of the boards. Evaluate their defects and decide if they will enhance or detract from your project. Think about how much of the original surface you want to retain. Find out what you can about the species and building source. As the late architect Louis Kahn might say, "What now, reclaimed wood?"

Remove the metal

Old nails are a reliable sign, besides old-growth color and grain, that wood is reclaimed. The softer nineteenth-century iron nail leaves its mark in the wood forever, oxidizing, or "bleeding," into the surrounding wood fibers, leaving ebonized marks.

The earliest specimens (pre-1820) are hand-forged, so valued by early Americans that old barns and houses would be dismantled or burned to recover the hardware. Families could spend nights pounding out nails for extra income. Even Thomas Jefferson declared, in 1795, "I am myself a nail-maker." (There was a nail factory at his Monticello plantation.) Both the Declaration of Independence and nails held the nation together. We generally see later-era "class A" and "class B" cut nails (c. 1820–1900). They were sheared from an iron plate. Steelmaking—the process invented in England by Henry Bessemer in 1855—led to the modern wire nails. But those nail types don't seem to appear until the turn of the century.

Nails and screws can be as stubborn as tree roots. If your wood will be encountering any woodworking tools, you'll have to pull them out. If you'll be using the lumber as is, this step may be optional, though surface removal or banging them in is recommended for safety and to avoid gouging.

After you secure the lumber onto a stable surface (sawhorses will do), visible nails are generally easy to remove with a claw hammer, although older cut nails or rusted nails can be brittle and break off, leaving a nail tip below the surface.

The search for hidden nails starts with the metal detector. We use the hand wands familiar at airport terminals, though others favor long beachcomber models. Some people wave away modern technology and make claim to a kind of sniffing out, gaining a feel from a knock on the board or catching glints of broken nail from the depths of a tiny hole. It sounds OK as a parlor game, but I wouldn't risk a planer blade.

The metal detector is guided down the board, floating a few inches above, until it signals a piercing chirp. We've never looked into what kind of magic in the wand picks up the ferrous chemistries below the wood surface. Holes can be clustered from nails entering at successive eras, leaving some refined detector work to locate the metal. In many instances, you can come at the hole from different directions to determine the strongest signal. All the detected holes can be circled with a piece of chalk before the next step, or you can remove each buried nail as you go.

Extraction calls for a small arsenal of hand tools, most of which are available in a basic woodworking shop or tool chest. The main ones are a hammer, a sharp chisel, a cat's paw, and a wonder of the trade, the crescent nail puller. The nail pullers are a one-trick pony, but well worth the investment. The old models are made of better steel and can often be found used on eBay. They're hard to break, but the tips, like the nose on pliers, can chip. So that's something to look out for in purchasing the tool. A means for sharpening chisels, either by hand or grind wheel, is also recommended.

We start by chiseling a tight circle around a hole where the metal detector sounds, until the top of a broken nail appears with enough space to pinch it with the claw of the nail puller or reach with a cat's paw. The chisel may come back into play over and over at the same hole. But, generally, the goal is to limit chisel gouges. Nail-pulling crews, like knitting circles, develop the dexterity and rhythm for the task.

Working a nail puller is relatively easy after practice. Its sharp tip is banged below the surface until it pinches the nail. You rock it back gently on a fulcrum while the nail eases out of its hole. For the nail, stationary for a century or more, it's an event. For the nail puller, it's not much of a party. If there's a craft to this step, it's in minimizing gouge marks.

Clean the wood

There can be dust, dirt, or light whitewash that has settled on the aged surface. Just washing the surface with soap and water can also have surprising results. For most reclaimed boards, a wire brush or, for larger jobs, a push broom are a good start. Power sanding, even with some pressure, can often knock down roughness without removing the character, and leave the surface safe to the touch. Saw marks often emerge better defined in the process. The exception would be gray barn siding, where any level of abrasion seems to remove the patina. We typically use a large mechanical brush or a powerful handheld model made by Makita. A lower cost option is to attach a brush to an angle grinder. You can experiment with different grit sizes, pressures, or degrees of skip-planing to achieve the desired aesthetic. Its best to keep it safe when removing paint, as old layers may contain lead. Gloves, a respirator, and a ventilated or outdoor space for the work are recommended.

Finishing

Centuries ago, wood finishing was the secret art of select craftsmen and guild members. A pamphlet written in 1515 under the title *The Olde and Annciente Ordinances Articles and Customes or Mistery; or, Occupation of the Painters* contains no formulas, just rules on how to keep the knowledge hidden. But gradually, chemists began to vie with artisans in the preparation of wood finishes. Explorers took naturalists with them on their travels around the world, and new dyes and resins were discovered. Bold and fancy cabinetry began to be crafted in Europe and Asia; often such work required special finishes, like a French polish, to express its aesthetic. And, as with YouTube today, the printing press began to make specialized knowledge widely available.

<
Squaring the edge of weathered barn siding.

By the early nineteenth century, the guild system in the United States was breaking down. American democracy inspired young apprentices to rebel against the overlord/master in the woodshop. And people were moving west, where skilled labor was scarce. Artisans who had specialized in one aspect of woodworking or furniture work (for example, joiners, sawyers, upholsterers, and finishers) had to become generalists. In 1827, the first American furniture finisher's manual was published, bringing specialized knowledge to general readers.

Even today, however, wood finishing, or its mastery, can still seem a mysterious amalgam of craft and science. The following is a brief review of finishes, both traditional and modern. A finish of some kind is often seen as essential to protect new wood from impacts, spills, and natural moisture changes and to add depth and color. But these are not always meaningful concerns or goals with reclaimed wood. Its natural subtle color tones may want to be preserved. Dings and scratches may be acceptable, if not welcome. Protection against spills, watermarks, and other stains may nonetheless be an issue. So, as in any finishing choice, one of the first considerations, along with cost and environmental issues, is the type of use the wood will get.

No finish

For some applications where a protective surface or an altering of color tone is not desired—an accent wall or shelving for dry goods, for instance—unfinished wood may be adequate. A large part of the value of reclaimed wood is its connection with history and the primal non-digital balance with modern life it offers, so it's hard to fault people who take a pass on a finish. For many aged woods, it could be said that time has imparted beauty and natural patina. Using finishes to bring out the grain of salvaged old-growth wood, or, alternatively, to lighten the tone with a pickling process, is best approached with caution. Testing your finish on scraps or the underside of a piece of reclaimed wood is always recommended as a first step.

Shellac

Shellac is an ancient finish made from a resin secreted by the tiny lac insect. It is natural, easy to apply and repair, and imparts rich luster and depth to wood. It can be considered short on protection when it comes to damage from heat and liquids. Eddie O'Donnell, a guitar maker who often applies a French polish, using thin layers of shellac, says he "once picked up a 1930s Gibson at a guitar museum down in Nashville, and the shellac and varnish finish still looked gorgeous for its era. Some of the things that people put shellac down for aren't always its downfall. Protection was not a problem." Most shellac is de-waxed, which allows for just about any other finish to stick on top. It is typically bought in flakes—ranging in tone from clear to amber to garnet (dark)—that must be dissolved in alcohol. The ratio of flakes to alcohol is called the "cut." Shellac is also available pre-mixed.

Beeswax

Beeswax is another ancient finish. It's often applied as a top coat, sometimes over shellac or oil finishes, and is then buffed. Many products employ the term wax, which most often refers to an unspecified percentage of beeswax, carnauba wax, or a synthetic variant. A beeswax finish is easy to make by mixing beeswax with mineral oil or natural vegetable oils. Wax adds a depth and luster, especially to aged woods, though it requires upkeep. Pigments can be added to waxes, further modifying or evening tones across aged boards without reducing the wood's natural look. Wax is most often applied to furniture these days, though the architect A. Hays Town (page 166) used amber-tinted wax on his heart-pine floors for decades, seemingly without performance issues.

Oil finishes

Oils like tung oil and boiled linseed oil, or ones spiked with hardeners like Danish oil, are excellent and time-honored finishes, although they will alter the original tones of wood by darkening the surface and accentuating the grain. Oils penetrate into wood fibers, which imparts a rich look that people often like. Whether to bring out the grain or maintain the original natural tones is a personal choice.

Like wax, an oil finish can help to even tones across aged boards if that is desired. For many rustic surfaces, we often skip-plane, or sand back, part

<
Skip-planed longleaf pine, unfinished on the left and treated with a traditional natural finish of shellac and beeswax on the right. This wood was salvaged from a former stable at 271 West 10th Street in New York City, where John Lennon is said to have done some recording.

of the original surface so that areas of the bare wood show through. Oils and waxes then beautifully enhance the soft transitions and tonal range across the board, an effect that at times feels like a bridging of eras (page 144). There is a wide range of oil finishes on the market, and many are manufactured with additional chemical hardeners, although oil finishes are not ideal for surface protection of wood.

Note that some reclaimed woods—longleaf pine is a prime example—slip toward orange when oil finishes are applied. This effect can be minimized with the newer low VOC but higher-priced water-based finishes like Bona Naturale or Loba 2K Invisible. It is not uncommon to add pigments to finishes to deepen the tones of longleaf pine, as in the historic grandstands at the Saratoga Springs racetrack or the Dunham School gym (page 213). Alternatively, a lye additive can be used to knock the orange hue down a notch, mimicking the bleached tones of Scandinavian wood treatments. We generally prefer to maintain the natural tones, in most instances, as they express the wood's old-growth qualities. Since our eyes are most sensitive to slight changes in intensity in the red/orange end of the color spectrum, what can seem pleasing in a warm-toned wood to one person may look garish to another. Used thoughtfully, finishes can help to manage warm tones.

Polyurethane

Polyurethane is a synthetic film finish that forms on top of the wood, and it's commonly used if a hard, protective topcoat is desired, typically for surfaces that expect traffic or abuse. It's available in a wide variety of oil- and water-based formulations that range from clear to amber and are easy to apply. At the extreme end of these protective finishes are resins and spray lacquers, which have become remarkably durable but can be toxic and expensive and generally must be applied by professional finishing shops. Durable finishes like these are often used when a pre-finished floor is needed. Pre-finishing wood generally adds a microbevel to the edges of the boards, which can give reclaimed wood flooring a fragmented and manufactured look, and industrial-strength topcoats can be so durable that refinishing in the future may call for aggressive measures. If you finish your floor on-site, after the wood is installed, you'll have better control of the tone and sheen.

Paint

A reverse finish, in a sense, is to paint the woods. Some apply this as counterintuitive approach to reclaimed, especially for distressed woods or surfaces they may find less attractive. Color highlights texture, cracks, nail holes, and other features, and painted wood can be effectively juxtaposed with its natural surface (page 177).

There is no blue without yellow, and without orange.

—Vincent van Gogh

>
clockwise from top left
Each panel is untreated on the lower left and finished on the upper right. Resurfaced Southeast Asian tropical hardwood from Japanese cargo ship crating, finished with tung oil; wormy chestnut barnwood, paneling grade, finished with an oil and varnish blend; Northeast softwood, original surface, from a barn, painted white and finished with polyurethane (Bona Naturale); Longleaf pine, character select grade, from 442 Greenwich Street, New York, finished with polyurethane (Loba 2K Invisible).

CHAPTER

05

DESIGNING
WITH
RECLAIMED
WOOD

Reclaimed Design

Salvaged wood is typically turned from structural to decorative use. Its makeover may involve a radical change in appearance, through a series of millwork processes, or it may simply call for a change in context— a ceiling beam reused as a bench, for example. In either instance, the material culture of a specific site is transformed through modern design.

But it can be challenging to incorporate reclaimed wood into décor, as many readers of this book may attest. Even as it delivers aesthetic rewards and the delight of conversation, winds continue to swirl around its use in design. How to use reclaimed wood sparks the questions about scale, narrative, context, clarity, and function that are the basic elements of any considered design vision. Although we have no formal design background, we have tried to offer examples in this chapter showing how reclaimed wood has been used in different styles, from traditional to modern.

All materials have a purpose in a good design, and in the case of reclaimed wood, this can be visual, tactile, or functional, or may speak to qualities that relate to history and culture. Here are some ideas about the role of reclaimed wood in design:

Context Salvaged woods, especially when locally sourced, are intimately connected to historical context and the genius loci, or the spirit of a place. A number of the projects we illustrate, like the New York City tech office (page 205), employ reclaimed wood to evoke local context without compromising materiality and performance.

Scale Wood products today are value engineered and come from smaller trees, without regard to the proportions of the spaces they're intended for. Reclaimed woods are often more naturally scaled to a space. The massive beams used for seating on the High Line (page 219) are an example.

Simplicity Old-growth reclaimed woods can be used to simplify and minimize design choices. A floor, for instance, typically a backdrop, can become a focal point, with exquisite figure, grain, and character. These qualities may even reduce the need for furnishings. The living room at the Glickman Schlesinger residence (page 159) is spare, but still filled with warmth and character.

Repetition Reclaimed wood's raw dimensional size and surface aging provides opportunities to use the same lumber in different applications within a space to unify and find rhythm. Brook Klausing's loft (page 165) raises the white-pine floors into stair treads and then finishes with a full-scale aged timber.

Accent Sometimes reclaimed wood works best as an accent. A little may go a long way when used as a focal point, as in the dining table at the Shobowale residence, set against the wide-plank oak floor (page 160) or the bathroom sink frame in a residence designed by the Jersey Ice Cream Co. (page 171).

<<
Wormy chestnut flooring at the Weeksville Heritage Center, Brooklyn (page 211).

<
Lye-washed, flat-sawn reclaimed longleaf pine flooring in a Queens, New York, row house (page 159) balances traditionalism and modernism.

Narrative The design stage of a project may focus on the visual and physical qualities of reclaimed wood, but when living with reclaimed wood, its history may assert itself, as in the Beggars Group's New York office (page 206) or the USA Pavilion at Expo Milano (page 216). This is reclaimed wood's intangible value.

Wabi-sabi Reclaimed woods are often said to be expressive of this Japanese tradition and philosophy. Wabi-sabi values the "imperfect, impermanent, and incomplete," according to Leonard Koren in his *Wabi-Sabi* (1994). "Things wabi-sabi are expressions of time frozen. They are made of material that are visibly vulnerable to the effects of weathering and human treatment. . . . Their nicks, chips, bruises, scars, dents, peeling, and other forms of attrition are a testament to histories of use and misuse." The architect A. Hays Town (page 166) was adroit in exploring these qualities of reclaimed wood.

Sustainability Sparing a living tree fosters positive feelings, and old-growth woods, especially, have depth and beauty that rewards the effort of renewing them. In considering the sustainable value of reclaimed wood, however, it's important to take into account the carbon cost in processing and transport.

The projects on the following pages range from residences, to commercial establishments, to cultural institutions, to infrastructure.

It used to be
a work horse,
now it's a
show piece.

—Bernard Gallagher

<
White oak timber

^
End-grain of heart pine showing
characteristic uneven growth rings
of light springwood and dense
amber summerwood.

1888 Passive House, Brooklyn

This 1888 wooden row house was restored in 2017 and certified to the PHI (Passive House Institute) energy standard. Passive house is a rigorous standard for energy efficiency. It was adopted in Europe in the 1990s, in response to global warming, and is now taking off in the United States. The strategy reduces energy use by up to 90 percent, with superinsulation, high-performance windows, and mechanical ventilation.

The project was undertaken by our own Sawkill Lumber with Paul A. Castrucci Architect and energy consultant David White. The house was stripped back to its bones and quite a bit of salvaged wood was introduced. The Victorian-era facade was restored with Douglas fir clapboard milled from Worcestershire sauce tanks and then charred, using a Japanese flame treatment known as *shou sugi ban* that extends the life of the wood. The back of the house is sheathed in tropical hardwoods from the Coney Island and Rockaway boardwalks (page 110). The windows are made from wine tank redwood (page 102). "Reclaimed woods and their history are part of the toolbox for design," says Annie Coggan, a design consultant at the project.

Brownstone, Bedford-Stuyvesant, Brooklyn

It has a classic Brooklyn brownstone facade. History also defines the interior, with antique wood floors made of Northeast softwoods (page 52) remilled from the siding of a potato barn in Hadley, Massachusetts. The untypical choice seems to fit with the high ceilings, exposed brickwork, and factory-style windows. The two apartments in the brownstone are defined by the surface treatment of the wood—original aged face versus skip-planed. The design expresses the sustainable outlook of its occupants, Adriane Birt, a crisis outreach specialist at Columbia University, and Michael Heller-Chu, a former officer for the United Nations. Adriane says of the repurposed wood, "its physical properties have become more important to my experience than its history."

Row House Restoration, Prospect Heights, Brooklyn

The owners of this "near" passive house restoration hadn't seen a South Carolina tobacco barn until one showed up on their stoop. Its red oak (page 66) timbers were remilled into flooring that covers the parlor space in a herringbone pattern, creating a dynamic refinement of its rugged nature. The husband is the director of the local green building council, and the wife is a graphic designer and art director; their use of reclaimed wood contributed to a sustainable design in collaboration with Thread Collective architects. The renovation combines antique, mid-century, and modern elements. All that's left of the tobacco barn is the occasional nail hole and the light smoky hues of the floorboards.

Architects Adam Glickman
and Lauren Schlesinger
renovated this 1910 Queens
row house. It was gutted,
with some details retained,
including patches of the
original narrow longleaf
pine (page 86) floor. They
installed pine of the same
era and species but milled
into wide planks from the
salvaged joists of an 1895
warehouse on Greenwich
Street in Manhattan. The
wood received a lye wash and
white-tinted oil finish. The
finish offers less protection
than polyurethane would, but
they like how it feels. "A three-
year-old daughter who likes to
throw toys adds to the patina,"
Adam related. "Though it's
subtle," says Lauren, "it never
looks scratched and has a
gradually aging patina. But
we wheeled a piano across
the room that created a deep
groove in the wood that is
less fun to look at."

State Street Row House, Brooklyn

This gut-renovated passive house gave as much attention to interior design as to the mechanical details. Tokumbo and Sheethal Shobowale, the husband and wife owners, who worked with architect Jane Sanders, had opposing aesthetic preferences: "I liked the clean look. She liked the character of aged wood," says he. The final choices in reclaimed wood flooring were a balance of both—wide-plank white oak (page 66) on the parlor floor and original surface cargo oak (page 114) in the bedroom. An elegant open-riser staircase has treads milled from oak barn timber finished to match the parlor floor. The heavier stress cracks are placed on the undersides of the treads, where they are visible from below. The dining table was made by Christopher Payan, an architect friend, from reclaimed joists salvaged at the property.

Auto Repair Shop, Brooklyn

A 1930 auto repair shop was gutted, leaving the facade on this residence built from the ground up. "It's nice to show something of what the neighborhood once was, even if not a beautiful garage," says owner JJ Snyder. "I like the sense of history around me, but also making it modern and functional." His wife, Becky Harvey, adds, "The fun part was pulling things together and making them work and correspond with the space." Working with FABR Studio + Workshop, they combined a structure of I-beams resting on concrete piers with soft finishes like rich magenta walls and oiled black-walnut baseboards. The Douglas fir (page 92) floors were milled from joists reclaimed during demolition.

Loft, Fort Greene, Brooklyn

The gut rehab of this loft space was the first interior project for Brook Klausing, who owns a company that designs and builds outdoor living spaces. The home is on the top floor of a four-story turn-of-the-century cast-iron building that was previously a hotel with a distant view of Manhattan. The twelve-inch antique white pine (page 82) floor boards were remilled from the structural joists of an 1898 building of the same scale and era on Manhattan's Upper East Side. The wide, long, light-toned planks met the scale and openness of the loft space, interacting with the bold I-beam construction and narrow-slatted, ebonized wood-paneled walls. Personal curiosities—birds, fish, an ax, driftwood, and arrows—conjure the wood's backstories, expressing qualities that the tall Southerner brings to the landscapes he designs in the North.

A. Hays Town House, Baton Rouge, Louisiana

Louisiana architect A. Hays Town (1903–2005) designed more than five hundred homes, combining Spanish, French, Creole, and Acadian elements of the South's rich architectural past, in the decades following World War II. He made unapologetic use of salvaged material, especially reclaimed wood—the native longleaf, cypress, and oak of the region, often sourced from nineteenth-century New Orleans houses. His style had an earthy quality, exhibiting benign neglect, with moss, vines, and fungi growing and clinging undisturbed to the sides of buildings.

He had notions of being an artist, following the lead of an uncle who had lived like a Beat poet in the 1920s. But Town had a stern father who disapproved of that career, and the young man found himself in architecture, where his sense of proportion, color, texture, and composition were put to use. He worked on modern structures until the 1960s, then took a decisive turn to residential clients; in working for them, he developed the style he is known for today.

Town's use of reclaimed southern longleaf pine (page 86), harvested a century or more ago and now making its way back to the region from demolished industrial structures around the United States, continues to define an ethos of building in the South.

Jersey Ice Cream Co. Projects

Tara Mangini and Percy Bright bring into their now well-known design work objects that are often overlooked and marginal, then "changed and repositioned." Their use of reclaimed wood is often sparing, establishing a focal point like a bold mantel or a bathroom sink frame built by Mr. Bright on site. A distressed wall section is reclaimed in place, set within a new wall. Or plank walls are painted, leaving an inky silhouette of grain and character marks. The firm's backstory starts at the Brimfield Flea Market in Massachusetts—Tara and Percy's fourth date, where the Jersey Ice Cream Co. stamp was reclaimed, to be used again and again.

Converted Factory, Geneva, New York

Brandon Miles Phillips and Amy May Phillips are furniture makers in Geneva, New York. Over the past twenty years, their company, Miles & May, which started in a Williamsburg, Brooklyn, cellar, moved first to a barn in upstate New York that burned down one night, and then to an abandoned cracker factory where they squatted, with a long view on restoration. As Amy says, "We work eighty hours a week, so we needed to live and work in a beautiful place. Some people like cars, we like space." Here, they live, work, and run an event and arts space. The ceiling boards were once the floor of a Pillsbury factory in Michigan that they picked up en route to making a delivery in Chicago. Their furniture often practices a similar reversal, with aged timbers planed smooth; material and history turned inside out and made modern.

Tiny House Restoration, Portland, Oregon

This tiny house on Sauvie Island north of Portland, built in the 1940s for shipyard workers, had "good bones and beautiful oaks," according to interior designer Jessica Helgerson. For its fourth reuse, it was restored by Helgerson and her husband, architect Yianni Doulis. Douglas fir (page 92) and other softwoods reclaimed at the property clad the interior. The raw woods were moderated: "We stained one wall and painted the rest white. It was just too much to have natural wood everywhere." Paint and stains are normally shunned when working with original surface–reclaimed woods, but when used with a designer's hand, we've seen these finishes highlight or silhouette aged character, like old-growth grain, nail holes, and stress cracks.

Bridge House,
Ann Arbor, Michigan

Located on a prairie in Ann Arbor, Michigan, Bridge House extends 120 feet between two low rising hills (page 180, bottom). Like many of Wilfred John Oskar Armster's residential buildings, it is designed for a difficult lot, with minimal changes to the natural landscape. The home blurs interior and exterior, with its window locations, open-air spaces, and a low horizontal form that appears nestled into the environment but is suspended just above. Reclaimed woods include often lower-valued softwood joists, ceiling paneling, and flooring remilled from stadium bleacher seats, providing light tones and subtle warmth to the space and a bridge to history and nature. Armster (1939–2019) developed a modernist style with an emphasis on sustainability. His Bridge House won the AIA Connecticut 2009 Design Award, being cited for its "taut simplicity." He once said, "Our quick existence is excited by forms and spaces that connect us to nature as well as protect us from nature."

^^
Nicola Armster's house
incorporates reclaimed and new
woods. Sinker cypress and red
gum from a Memphis, Tennessee,
building contrast with white
cedar and a steel I-beam.

^
Heidi Armster's house includes
re-surfaced antique spruce joists
from New York City.

Wilfred John Oskar Armster Architect

Author Klaas Armster discusses his late father's work.

What stands out most for you in Wil Armster's work?

My father's work often referenced bridges, walls, and holes. His houses were designed for difficult places, like the project in Ann Arbor that spans rolling hills. As much as anything, he didn't want to change the landscape, and some projects have large trees that grow through them or do not disrupt the tall grasses of a prairie. Although the exteriors of his buildings, with their simple, strong forms, garnered the most attention, it was the interiors that were most impressive to me, always so light and private and so unexpected coming from the outside. And he managed to produce excellent buildings without spending a lot.

How did he use reclaimed woods?

When he was building Bridge House, there was very little demand for reclaimed wood that was not rustic. We resawed 3 x 5-inch boards from a tobacco barn, and he was happy with narrow material and with the fact that it was light, as he didn't like brown board. There were also bleacher seat boards that were clear and loose-grained, and those were used for the floors. He'd often use types of woods that he could get cheaper and would work on a low budget for a project.

You have a large and close family. How did that influence his work?

He liked to include his family in his projects. My brother, Sven, often helped with designs or did millwork. My sister Heidi, a photographer, often shot the buildings. My other sister Nicola worked at the family mill, Wood, Steel & Glas, where she milled white cedar for the projects. I supplied reclaimed lumber. And my mom did a little of everything. We were all involved in some way. It was always that way with him.

^
top to bottom
Nicola's House, Guilford, Connecticut; Heidi's House, Easton, Connecticut; Bridge House, Ann Arbor, Michigan.

House, Hollywood, California

A barnwood facade in the Hollywood Hills sounds more like a movie set than a million-dollar listing. In the late 1800s, the area was a thriving farm community, so barnwood is part of the area's origin story, even if they're not cladding the iconic Hollywood sign with it. The woods for this house were sourced from a Wisconsin dairy barn. Costs are higher for wood from historical barns, but "it's hard to mimic nature and time" says Eric Fried at the project. Barnwood mania has given rise to imitations across the country. It's also not uncommon to see a mist of color applied to reclaimed woods, which can even color tones for some design applications. On this California hill, the original weathered gray and whitewashed boards are maintained by their exposure to the sun.

Bunkhouse, Upstate New York

A "bunkhouse" is typically basic housing of workers, visitors, or campers. The Bunkhouse is inspired by that essential idea of daily life outdoors. Located in upstate New York, it is surrounded by fifty acres of wood, fields, and a brook. The ground-up construction by Material Design Build incorporates large windows, loft ceilings, and natural materials, including white shiplap and reclaimed timbers sourced from a Pennsylvania barn formerly owned by the founders of the Mack Trucks company. The hewn barnwood is offset by the acid-stained concrete floors and exposed steel stairs. "We were trying not to put too much wood into the space, so that the old timber pops," says project architect Armin Zomorodi.

Artist's House, Long Island

This former barn in eastern Long Island was stripped back to its hewn timbers to create a contemporary living space. Adding Northeast softwood (page 52) timbers from nearby structures and employing discreet metal joinery work, artist David Salle and architect Michael Haverland were able to keep the spirit of this old barn alive and vital. Juxtaposed against the white walls and concrete floor, the beams contribute warmth, texture, and scale. It's a well-ordered living environment that is adjacent to a studio where the artist creates his work.

Butterfly House, Jackson, Wyoming

"A house on the top of a hill in Jackson Hole has to have some weight to it," says architect Larry Pearson, "but this house has lightness, too. It's that combination that intrigues us." Pearson was an early protege of architect Jonathan Foote, who also founded On Site Management, the firm that built the home. The award-winning house reflects a direction that is combining Western vernacular with modernism. Interiors mix rustic raw materials with steel and glass. Soft grayish ponderosa pine and Douglas fir boards reclaimed from regional fencing clad walls and ceilings, and heavy eastern hemlock (page 76) timbers from Pennsylvania barns have been fashioned into furniture. The floors are reclaimed oak (page 66). The different woods are meant to echo the colors and textures of the surrounding landscape, with the spectacular Teton Range in the distance.

^^
House, Big Sky, Montana.
Hewn timbers, sourced from
a homestead cabin, retain
their original dovetail joinery.

^
The fireplace and a painting of
Chinese calligraphy, from the
owner's family history, are at the
hearth of the home. Floors are
milled from reclaimed American
chestnut.

Jonathan Foote
Architect

When did you start using reclaimed wood?

My brother called, and it was the early 1960s. I was living in the East, and I'd recently graduated from architecture school at Yale. And he asked me to design a house for him in Montana. There were these old homestead cabins, and they were falling down, full of shit and claw marks and bullet holes and all that. And he asked if there was anything we could do with them. I took one look and said, "We can have a hell of a good time with this."

The first clients were affluent folks in Jackson Hole. The use of the old woods caught on like wildfire. It went full cycle from being a poverty measure [laughs], if you will, to an elegant statement.

What is the value of using reclaimed wood?

The example of a bullet hole in the old timber of a house in Jackson, Wyoming . . . It invokes a karmic response from everybody at the table when the owner points out, "That was a bullet hole estimated to be from 1860." It's carrying with it a life that was vital and real, and was brought into a more civilized part of the world. There's a whole lot I couldn't know, and that the bullet hole knows everything about. What forced some guy to pull a

gun and shoot a bullet, which ended up in this timber? Maybe he was shooting at a grizzly bear and missed. Maybe an Indian raid. Maybe a pissed-off wife shooting at her husband [laughs]. Who knows. But that's where the excitement comes in, both in the wilderness and the use of old materials.

How do you use reclaimed materials?

There can be an over-rustication of the old materials. Most builders miss the importance of balance, of proportion and scale, and the way materials come together, which is purely instinctual. But when it's put together well and thoughtfully, and there is a patina system, people see it, and they fall in love with it. You have to walk a real fine line between sentimentality and the love of history. The way I've handled it with buildings is that I choreographed the flow of space in the buildings, so that they really celebrate the natural environment. Maybe a mountain range that's a hundred miles away, but it's been played into the theme and materials from the time you arrive at the house to the time you leave it. That's what really allows the old woods to be celebrated, because they are part of that story, and part of that love affair between nature and civilization.

Who are influences that stand out?

Vincent Scully and Louis Kahn were great mentors of mine. As an architect, Louis Kahn really made me aware of the subtleness, and the modern feel of antiquity, in bringing spatial flow, the use of light, and changing volumes. He was such a protean interpreter of the elements of architecture. And he made me keenly aware of the importance in trying to be honest about these things. About the way two materials come together. Do they kiss or do they crash? That's the modern dimension of these old materials.

City Point,
Brooklyn, New York

City Point is a large
commercial development
in downtown Brooklyn,
with a public thruway built
above a transit hub. The
welcoming interior, designed
by Gensler, incorporates
dynamic electronic displays
and commercial tenants like
Joybird and Trader Joe's.
Reclaimed wood softens the
commercial elements in the
large space. The walls are a
harmonious arrangement of
the Coney Island boardwalk
(page 110) and Japanese
cargo tropical hardwoods
(page 114), old-growth
cypress vinegar-tank wood
(page 98), and gray barn
siding in slightly varied widths
and thicknesses (page 10–11).
A wash coat prevents the
contrasts in tone from being
severe.

The siting of 1 Hotel Brooklyn Bridge within Brooklyn Bridge Park was a heated community issue. The project has gained accolades since completion. The use of 3 x 8-inch wood fins resawn from Pennsylvania barn timbers for the hotel's bold exterior rain screen, by Rogers Marvel Architects, helped connect the building to the park's master plan by Michael Van Valkenburgh Associates. The park, which utilized pine and fir timbers salvaged from the National Cold Storage building, a late nineteenth-century building formerly on the site, rolls down the bank of the East River, with walking paths, fields, ball courts, and boat docks.

Freemans Sporting Club Barbershop, Lower East Side, New York City

The original Freemans Sporting Club Barbershop in New York's historic Lower East Side offered a tribute to the heritage of its neighborhood. The molding profiles were traditional. The wood was antique quality. But the design, crafted by Friends + Family, was only half nostalgia. The Northeast softwoods (page 52) were salvaged and remilled with nail holes and stress cracks. The light tones helped to brighten the space, which got little natural light. Typically, the pale inner boards of aged softwood joists are sacrificed for the rustic-faced outer boards, popular for paneling. Here, their subtle and light figure, and the revealed signs of their history, were celebrated, and these often-scorned pieces were transformed by intricate millwork into a high end cut.

Bareburger Restaurant, Chelsea, New York City

Bareburger locations combine the recycled, reclaimed, and repurposed along with selected new restaurant furnishings. The evolving variations on the theme have an anything-goes look; a pleasing but unassuming balance, like the ingredients in their popular burgers. A medley of barn siding is set against neutral-toned benches. Scrap-wood chairs, tiles, glass lighting, and tin plate create a mash-up of colors, materials, and patina. The reclaimed floors best reflect the brand. They're made from a collection of old-growth hardwoods that may include beech, maple, elm, oak, and hickory, but could also turn up the odd sassafras, poplar, or red gum plank that can be found in an old barn.

Gold Cash Gold Restaurant, Detroit

The name of Gold Cash Gold, a restaurant in Detroit, is a play on the site's previous use as a pawn shop. The reclaimed wood decor isn't far off, if you're counting old-growth rings like gold karats. The centerpiece in the floor is a half-court emblem from the hard maple gymnasium floor (page 118) of a local school—a spread eagle with dangling claws. The ceiling is an installation of narrow wood lathe—thousands of pieces carefully extracted from the walls during renovation, then cleaned, trimmed, and nailed into a herringbone pattern. Anyone who has done that painstaking salvage and reinstallation work before is raising a glass to it at the bar.

Arlo Hotel,
New York

We thought the developers would trash the idea of salvaging wood from one of their properties for use at another—a stylish Midtown Manhattan hotel. We were wrong. The Northeast softwoods (page 52), exuding manure and gas scents, and layered with horse piss and a half-inch of grime, came out of a nineteenth-century stable that had been turned into a parking garage as cars replaced horses. Many samples later, the owners' and the design team had arrived at a uniquely distressed floor, installed in a two-toned chevron pattern.

Tech Office,
New York

In the planning stage of an office renovation, the staff at a large tech company were asked, "Where do you want to go when you leave the office?" About 60 percent answered, "The park." The response helped drive design to "push things the other way, where the high tech and ethereal things we work with are combined with softer, more natural materials," explains Aleksey Lukyanov-Cherny of the architecture firm, Situ Studio. Modular work desks and circadian lighting systems that get warmer toward evening combine with the color pop of modern furniture and reclaimed wood. The factory maple flooring (page 94) evokes the history of innovation and industry in the area. Barn oak (page 66), milled but still rustic, serves in quieter pods and hidden rooms where people retreat to recharge.

The Beggars Group, SoHo, New York

The Beggars Group helped propel some of the great punk bands of recent eras. Working with Cycle Architecture + Planning, they mostly used reclaimed maple from a circa 1895 Edison factory (page 94) for their offices on a landmark corner of New York's SoHo neighborhood. The three-inch factory maple bears marks from industrial carts and machinery, paints, fluids, and mothballs, all encased under a hard film finish, and pays tribute to the roots of recorded music and rage.

Whole Foods,
Gowanus, Brooklyn

Whole Foods often incorporates regionally sourced reclaimed woods into their design as part of the company's ethos of sustainability. When they opened their first Brooklyn location in the Gowanus neighborhood, they took eco-practices a step further, with a rooftop farm, wind turbines, and deep reclamation. A central feature was reclaimed wood from the Coney Island boardwalk (page 110), employed for wall cladding, stair treads, checkout dividers, tables, and produce bins. Recent locations in the borough are conspicuously absent of the same rugged beauty.

Etsy Headquarters, Brooklyn

Etsy headquarters is a reflection of the e-commerce website, being well-crafted, eclectic, and eco-friendly; to express those values and enhance the working environment, they've brought in plants, a newly popular element of sustainable office design. The Greenery NYC, a Brooklyn-based indoor landscaping company, installed freestanding and wall-mounted planter boxes clad in reclaimed woods, alternating original and resurfaced textures. The old woods were sourced from a building in Tin Pan Alley, Manhattan's former pop music hub. Backstories have been important to Etsy. One cladding installation used hemlock (page 76) from an Edison warehouse, favored over reclaimed woods linked to rainforest loss. We've seen salvaged wood connected to heavy issues, like the crating of nuclear parts, and grisly histories, including a double homicide. Not everyone wants to live with such woods.

Weeksville Heritage Center, Weeksville, Brooklyn

African American slaves in New York were emancipated in 1827. Many headed to Weeksville, Brooklyn, gaining land and voting rights. The Weeksville Heritage Center celebrates that "strong pioneering model of freedom." Matter Practice, the designer of the updated exhibition space, utilized reclaimed wormy chestnut (page 56) for flooring. The boards, salvaged from a Pennsylvania barn, speak to heartbreaking loss and reclamation, like the history on the wall. Chestnut has a handsome open-grained figure, similar to oak, but is moderately softer. At the entrance to the museum, staff member Marvin Hickman designed a shelving unit for the gift shop that revived a heavily distressed barn threshing floor.

Dunham School,
Baton Rouge, Louisiana

The longleaf pine installed as stadium seating at the Dunham School gym has roots in the South, where it was cut as lumber in the 1800s, but then was sent north. The Louisiana homecoming is thanks to the generosity and vision of a board member at the school. Reclaimed longleaf (page 86) is a practical, though high-budget, choice for what is generally a utility application. Here it's been stained a rich brown ochre— a traditional practice. The deeper tone is set in contrast to the lighter maple basketball court. The long, wide planks are a performance fit as well, sturdy enough for a full house of stomping fans, as when the Dunham basketball team won a state championship in 2018.

Columbia University Manhattanville Campus, New York City

Columbia University undertook a multi-block transformation along the western edge of Harlem in New York City beginning in 2014. Demolished in the process was a brick warehouse at 3251 Broadway, which had housed a range of enterprises through the years, including the Universal Shock Eliminator Company in the 1920s. They produced shock absorbers for cars and for tanks seeing World War I service, and patented the car bumper in 1927. The Columbia project reclaimed wood from the warehouse for exterior benches. The longleaf pine (page 86) was cut into a relatively clear vertical grade to increase exterior performance. The design introduced another material layer at the site and echoes the grid patterns in the adjacent building designed by Renzo Piano Building Workshop.

USA Pavilion, Expo Milano, Milan, Italy

Expo Milano, held in Milan, Italy, in 2015, centered around the theme "Feeding the Planet, Energy for Life." The USA Pavilion presented "American Food 2.0." Designed by Biber Architects, it featured a vertical farm, smart glass roof for midday shade, and food venders lined along a remilled Coney Island boardwalk (page 110). In a case like this, the sustainability of reclaimed wood is somewhat undercut by the environmental cost of shipping it overseas, but other values come into play: "It had such incredible symbolic value," said James Biber of the boardwalk, "like a museum piece; a piece of American history." The next stop for the boardwalk is Hamburg, Germany.

The High Line, New York City

The High Line is a one-and-a-half-mile elevated park built on a former New York Central Railroad elevated line. The park was a collaboration between James Corner Field Operations, Diller Scofidio + Renfro, and Piet Oudolf. Designed as a "living system" in 2009, it has become an icon of contemporary landscape architecture. Reclaimed woods factored into the sustainable elements of the project, as seen here in the bold pyramidal seating made from Douglas fir (overleaf and page 92) recovered from a World War II–era hanger in New Jersey. Bench seating employs durable tropical hardwoods, transformed from another celebrated edge of the city, the Coney Island boardwalk (left and page 110).

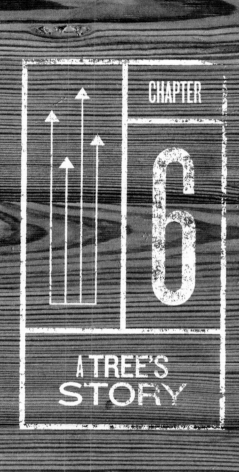

CHAPTER

6

A TREE'S
STORY

A Tree's Story

The themes of this book can be brought together in the imagined story, drawing on natural history, historical facts, and general lore, of one longleaf pine tree. Our tree sprouts in the 1540s, in what is today George County, Mississippi, between the Pascagoula River and the border of Alabama, although it might have originated anywhere there were longleaf forests across the South over several hundred years. We'll follow this tree from those roots, to an 1882 building in Lower Manhattan, to the places where its wood has been reclaimed in the twenty-first century.

Longleaf once grew from North Carolina to the tip of Texas and south to the Florida Panhandle—the largest forested lands in North America. A near monoculture, it is said to have reversed the rules of most forests, creating an alliance with fire, drawing light to the forest floor, and posing as grass. There is little visual record of its passage. One wishes there had been late nineteenth-century photographers intrepid enough to capture these forests before they were decimated. But there are glowing descriptions, like that by eighteenth-century British naturalist William Bartram, from his *Travels* (1791): "We next entered a vast forest of the most-stately Pine trees that can be imagined, planted by nature . . . rousing the faculties of the mind, awakening the imagination by its sublimity, and arresting every active, inquisitive idea, by the variety of the scenery."

Studies show that longleaf pines produce a tremendous output of cones in about a seven-year cycle. By October, dry winds open the cones, sending

<<
Select grade longleaf pine.

<
Longleaf saplings, South Carolina.

>
Map showing distribution of longleaf pine and Cuban pine. USDA, 1891.

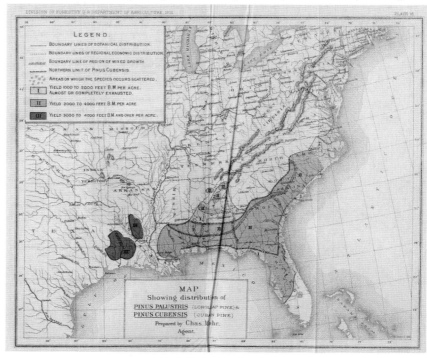

the winged seeds spiraling to earth. Slightly smaller than a sunflower seed and sought by just about every seed-eating animal in the forest, they need to germinate quickly. About a month later, the ones that escape hungry wildlife put down roots in the moist, mineral-rich soil. Seemingly overnight, a pair of two-inch-long needles emerge like magic from the earth. Longleaf seedlings are frugal consumers of water and light and indistinguishable from a clump of grass, unlike a young tree. For several years, growth happens underground, where the grass-stage tree's taproot penetrates three feet down, with lateral roots of similar length. Eventually, if conditions favor the tree, the longleaf sapling enters the "rocket stage" of its growth, reaching twenty feet in height in as little as five years. It doesn't bother to grow limbs. The starches it has been storing power it upward in adolescent spurts of overflowing green hair. At safe height, it begins to grow like other types of pine.

At about seventy years, into the early seventeenth century, our tree is only four inches thick. It grows straight and strong, its branches naturally pruned. And it then begins to expand in girth, developing its signature branches, intricate wrought-iron curls across a flat open crown. It builds up heavy resinous summer wood, an evolutionary defense against fungi, bacteria, and insects.

Over the next two hundred years areas of the longleaf pine belt are periodically scourged with fire, and, less frequently, decimated by hurricanes and tornadoes. Our tree, like all longleaf pines, has excellent fire resistance. Two hundred years into its maturity, an ivory-billed woodpecker excavates a cavity in our tree's old-growth trunk to feed on insects under the bark. Wildflowers—bog pinks, briar, and vanilla plants—float out of the savannah-like wire grass that covers the forest floor. At times, strong winds move through the longleaf canopy with a roar. Native American hunters in deerskin pass under the tree. Much later, it hears the distant guns of the Civil War. Our tree is now 330 years old, as vigorous as younger trees. Its sapwood pulses with life. The longleaf continues to add fine rings to its trunk and looks like it could live forever.

But it doesn't survive a logging crew that arrives around 1880.

At the time it was felled, our longleaf was, at twenty inches in diameter and one hundred and twenty feet high, a prime saw log. Had it been five years earlier, the "choppers" would have arrived with axes. But something more

< Flora and fauna of the longleaf forest: ivory-billed woodpecker (believed to be extinct), fox squirrel, corn snake, and purple blazing star.

^ Crosscutting a longleaf pine, Columbia, South Carolina. Photograph by E. S. Shipp, earlier twentieth century.

efficient was now available—the two-man crosscut saw. It's arrival was an event, with the people of the piney woods traveling for miles just to see how the new tool worked. Let's say that our tree was cut by loggers working for Calvin Taylor at the time. They made about a dollar a day and considered ten logs a good day's work. They would have loaded it onto a wheeled ox cart with broad, thick treads, an improvement on traditional wheels recently introduced to the region by Usan Vaughan, a former slave from Pearlington, Mississippi.

Kids as young as twelve ran alongside the load, cracking long deerskin whips, or "poppers," just for the fun of it. Arriving at the bank of Red Creek, our tree might have been sold to West Fairley, an African American timber merchant, who had it branded and readied for rafting. Running logs was said to be the best loved of all the loggers' tasks, carrying a spirit of adventure for old and young. Swift currents assisted Fairley's crew, using jam poles and peaveys, to guide the load down Red Creek to the Pascagoula River and the sorting booms and "bull pens" closer to the mills. Fairley might have sold the logs to Lorenzo N. Dantzler, a mill man who would later loan Fairley funds to buy timberland from the state.

In the 1880s, only logs without defects were marketable. Timber had to be free of knots and sapwood, and a large volume was rejected or sold at lower prices. Our log passed, having less than an inch of sap wood, and moved to the Dantzler mill at Moss Point, Mississippi.

The tree was milled into the three-inch-by-fifteen-inch dimensional lumber that would be used to frame 351 Broadway, more than one thousand miles to the north. Dantzler's massive circular saws cut more than ten million additional board feet that same year. A large volume of that output went overseas, especially to Germany, where there was heavy demand for "pitch pine," sought for exterior uses like wagons, window casings, freight cars, and other woodwork.

The Hudson River Mill and Lumber Company in New York City, run by Dexter Newell and his sons, was in communication with an agent based in New Orleans named Oremus Bushnell. Bushnell made the rounds through Mobile and Pascagoula, managing logistics and negotiating prices for a number of Northern firms. In April of 1882, he secured a large shipment of the southern pine at 12 cents per cubic foot for the Hudson River Mill, and we'll say that our tree was part of the deal.

In August, the boards were shoved on rollers into an opening in the hull of a large schooner. After sailing through the Gulf of Mexico and then up the East Coast, she docked at a pier in the Hudson River, just a few blocks from the company's lumberyard at "the foot of West 19th St." in Manhattan. There, the pine lumber would have been stacked high, with narrow cross sticks between each row for air flow. It joined longleaf lumber from the Carolinas, Florida, and Georgia, along with northern pine, hemlock, and spruce.

On an October morning in 1882, perhaps, the twenty-two-foot-long boards from our tree, still amber hued and looking freshly sawn, were loaded onto a horse cart (made of the same southern pine) and roped down. The streets of the

Gilded City were cobblestoned and covered with horse manure. Hogs roamed freely. Not long after dawn, the longleaf arrived at 351 Broadway, at the corner of Leonard Street.

A new commercial loft was replacing an early 1800s–era building at the address. A daguerreotype salon with large windows facing the busy street was planned for the second floor. Lower Broadway was still a destination for portraits, and the Civil War photographer Matthew Brady had had a salon next door a while earlier. The city was growing and reinventing itself. Lumber from our tree would frame dozens of businesses at 351 Broadway over the century—photography studios and a dealer of straw hats, a perfume company and a wallpaper outlet, book publishers and a camping goods store, and a luncheonette. It witnessed fires, parades, and robberies, as the neighborhood went in and out of fashion.

In 2015, the building was bought by Toll Brothers, a national real-estate developer, and slated for demolition. Our tree, severed from its roots for a hundred and thirty years, had set down new ones in the city's fabric, becoming what P. T. Barnum, whose legendary American Museum had been just a few blocks to the south until it burned down in 1865, might have called "an extraordinary object of nature and history." Demolition in the summer of 2017 saw the longleaf lumber lowered by rope, just as it had gone up, and hand-loaded onto Jimani Belle's long flatbed truck. When it reached the reclaimed lumber yard in Springfield, Massachusetts, it was just about four hundred and seventy years since it had sprouted.

Some of the reclaimed longleaf returned to the South in 2016, and its reuse as gymnasium bleachers at the Dunham School (page 213) in Baton Rouge, Louisiana, is a great example of how the valued and rich legacy of the southern forest can be honored.

And in the fall of 2018, some boards were milled into a traditional grade of vertical-grain flooring for the ongoing restoration of the Seventh Regiment Armory, also known as the Park Avenue Armory, at 643 Park Avenue in Manhattan, built in the Gothic Revival style in 1880.

The reclaimed longleaf that had grown in the South and then went North in 1882 ultimately kept roots in both places. In that way, it continued on with the life of a tree—a unity of earth and sky, fire and rain.

Salvaging lumber can't save the forests that were decimated in the twentieth century. But reclamation inspires regeneration. The living tree's uncanny grandeur is echoed in the old-growth grain and figure of the reclaimed planks. Environmental and economic arguments make increasing sense. At stands in the Red Hills of Georgia or Baldwin County, Alabama, or Bruce, Florida, or the Mobile Botanical Gardens, longleaf forests are being carefully brought back, and reclaimed.

<
The last days of 351 Broadway, 2015. In high-density zones, old buildings come down the way they went up, by hand. The longleaf beams are being cut away from the walls for reclamation.

v
Design architects Herzog & de Meuron and executive architects PBDW, working with Madera Trade, brought 351 Broadway and southern longleaf into the future at the Park Avenue Armory. A century ago, it was impossible to find old-growth longleaf to restore the floor. In 2018, the job was accomplished with reclaimed wood.

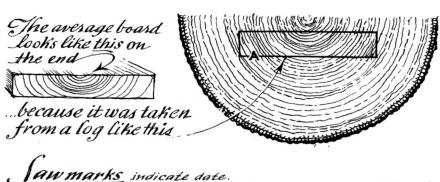

The average board looks like this on the end

...because it was taken from a log like this

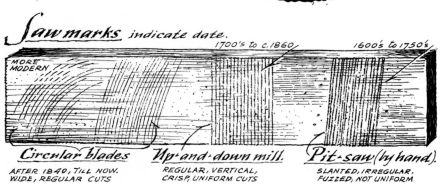

Saw marks indicate date.

1700's to c.1860

1600's to 1750's

MORE MODERN

Circular blades
AFTER 1840, TILL NOW. WIDE, REGULAR CUTS

Up-and-down mill.
REGULAR, VERTICAL, CRISP, UNIFORM CUTS

Pit-saw (by hand).
SLANTED, IRREGULAR, FUZZED, NOT UNIFORM

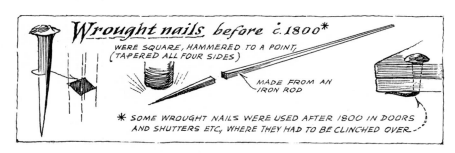

*Wrought nails before c.1800**

WERE SQUARE, HAMMERED TO A POINT, (TAPERED ALL FOUR SIDES)

MADE FROM AN IRON ROD

* SOME WROUGHT NAILS WERE USED AFTER 1800 IN DOORS AND SHUTTERS ETC., WHERE THEY HAD TO BE CLINCHED OVER

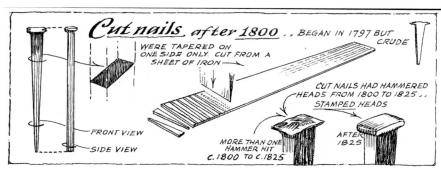

Cut nails after 1800 .. BEGAN IN 1797 BUT CRUDE

WERE TAPERED ON ONE SIDE ONLY. CUT FROM A SHEET OF IRON

CUT NAILS HAD HAMMERED HEADS FROM 1800 TO 1825 .. STAMPED HEADS

FRONT VIEW

SIDE VIEW

MORE THAN ONE HAMMER HIT c.1800 TO c.1825

AFTER 1825

<<
Young longleaf pine forest, South Carolina.

^
Illustrations by Eric Sloane showing how a flat-sawn board is cut from a log; how saw marks can be used to date wood; and how different types of nails can be used to date wood.

Glossary

Board Foot
A unit of lumber that is 12 x 12 inches square and 1 inch thick.

Check
A small or large crack or fissure in the wood surface that can occur within wood fibers over time, as the wood expands and contracts in response to seasonal humidity. A common feature of reclaimed woods and a testament to their strength and endurance.

Cut Nail
A nineteenth-century nail with a tapered rectangular form and blunt point. It was cut from a thin rolled sheet of iron or steel.

Dirty Top
A term often used in the southern United States to describe heart-pine floors that retain the aged original surface.

End-Grain
The grain, such as the mesmerizing and dense rings of heart pine, that is revealed when wood is crosscut.

Ferrous-Stained
A reclaimed wood surface after contact with iron or steel that was attached or embedded. The marks left can result from the hoops that secure a storage tank or from the bleed of a brittle pre-steel iron nail.

Growth Ring
The layer added to a tree trunk in a single growing year, composed of lighter-toned and faster-growing springwood and darker, slower growth summerwood.

Flat-Sawn
Timber that is saw-cut straight through the wood and typically exhibits a cathedral-like figure pattern. Most reclaimed wood is flat-sawn in the style of its historical cut and preserving the natural figure.

Hand-Hewn
Old barn timber that was originally cut with an ax and exhibits heavily textured "hewn" marks along the surface.

Hardwoods
Generally, deciduous trees that have broad leaves, in contrast to the conifers or softwoods. The term does not always reference the hardness of the wood. For instance, the hardness rating of longleaf pine is similar to that of red oak.

Heartwood
The hard, inner spine of a tree, made dense and generally darker by the accumulation of tannin, gums, resins, and pigments. It is more durable and decay-resistant than sapwood. Reclaimed antique woods are nearly all heartwood.

Moisture Content
The percentage of water in wood. Fresh-cut logs are about 30 percent water. Antique wood that has air-dried for a century has generally reached equilibrium with the surrounding atmosphere, but benefits from further drying for modern applications.

Nail Bleed
Old iron cut nails decompose within lumber, spreading into the wood fibers and leaving a blackened ferrous mark around the nail hole.

Old Growth
A tree or forested area that has never been felled, harvested, or cleared, and has been left to mature. The trees can be hundreds of years old. Nearly all reclaimed woods from the nineteenth century were logged from old-growth forests.

Patina
Used to describe the layer that forms on reclaimed wood through decades of exposure and wear.

Saw Mark
The shape and angle of the cut can be read to determine the type of saw used, and can be an indication of the wood's era.

Skip-Planed
A process in which the face of an aged or antique board is planed to a varied degree, revealing highlights of its underlying wood grain while retaining an aged patina. This surface treatment goes by various names in the industry.

Softwoods
Cone-bearing trees, most of which retain needles in winter. Softwoods evolved on earth millions of years before broadleaf hardwoods, and have a simpler cell structure.

Tongue and Groove
The most common wooden flooring or paneling today, in which adjacent boards are joined by means of interlocking ridges and grooves along their edges.

Vertical Grain or Comb Grade
The grain pattern on the face of a board where the figure runs in a parallel pinstripe formation from one end of the board to the other. Often found in antique softwoods like longleaf pine or Douglas fir.

Wire-Brushed
Aged paneling and flooring that has been mechanically brushed to remove dust and other particles from the surface, while retaining the old wood's aged color and texture.

Wormy
A description often applied to American chestnut infested by chestnut weevils that left the trunks filled with wormholes and discolorations. Chestnut trees dying of chestnut blight were felled for their lumber, which was still usable, often for barns. The tiny and precise wormholes have, ironically, become a cherished characteristic of this rare wood.

Further Reading

These books have been like trail markers in our reading about the woods we reclaim. They can help unearth the deeper back stories and illuminate the present. If you wish to research local wood, regional libraries and archival resources are, of course, the best to explore.

Finch, Bill, Beth Maynor Young, Rhett Johnson, and John C. Hall. *Longleaf: Far As the Eye Can See: A New Vision of North America's Richest Forest*. Chapel Hill: University of North Carolina Press, 2012.

Hough, Romeyn B, and Klaus Ulrich Leistikow. *The Woodbook: The Complete Plates*. Los Angeles: Taschen, 2013

Koren, Leonard. *Wabi-Sabi for Artists, Designers, Poets & Philosophers*. Point Reyes, California: Imperfect Publishing, 2008.

Littell, Harry, and Ronald E. Ostman. *Wood Hicks and Bark Peelers: The Photographic Legacy of William T. Clarke*. University Park: Pennsylvania State University Press, 2016.

Maloof, Joan. *Among the Ancients: Adventures in the Eastern Old-Growth Forests*. Washington, DC: Ruka Press, 2011.

Peattie, Donald Culross. *A Natural History of North American Trees*. San Antonio, Texas: Trinity University Press, 2013.

Pike, Robert E. *Tall Trees, Tough Men: An Anecdotal and Pictorial History of Logging and Log-Driving in New England*. New York: W. W. Norton & Co., 1999.

Rutkow, Eric. *American Canopy: Trees, Forests, and the Making of a Nation*. New York: Scribner, 2012.

Sloane, Eric. *A Reverence for Wood*. Hawthorne, California: BN Publishing, 2014.

Tudge, Colin. *The Tree: A Natural History of What Trees Are, How They Live, and Why They Matter*. New York: Broadway Books, 2007.

Wohlleben, Peter. *The Hidden Life of Trees: What They Feel, How They Communicate—Discoveries from a Secret World*. Vancouver and Berkeley: Greystone Books, 2015.

Acknowledgments

To the memory of our parents,

Sarah and Wilfred Armster
Irene and Milton Solomon

Lower Manhattan seemed an unlikely place to start a book on old-growth forests. It was where we first met the publisher. But there were also intimate connections at the site. An early mill, powered by wind, had been erected nearby in 1623, and Klaas's ancestor seems to have had a hand in its operation. I'd fallen into this salvage work a few blocks east at an 1832 warehouse. The book also seemed unlikely, as far as we'd never worked on one and imagined its being a raw prospect, like the wood.

So we're thankful to Eric Himmel, our editor at Abrams, for seeing potential in the material, and for the care and focus needed to see it through to completion. "The Art of Books," we learned, is no simple tagline.

We are thankful to Jane Creech. She embraced the idea for the book when we first met at Brooklyn Designs in 2016. She has been more than a pu blishing agent in shaping the content and keeping us on track.

We are thankful to have worked with Michel Arnaud. His vision and experience with the camera seemed to extract something fresh and vital in the old woods, as with trees, woodworking machinery, and modern design.

We are thankful to Debra Castellano for passionately editing the text in the initial stages. Thank you to Jane Bobko for her indispensable copy editing. Toby Gardner shared valuable critical review and revisions. Still, errors and omissions are ours alone.

Thank you to graphic designer Peter Ahlberg. He knew what to kill and made bold elegant design.

We are thankful to the people who work hard at every stage, from dismantling to millwork. Special thanks to Ken and Cindy Strout, Cesar Garcia, Carlos Orellana, Brian Hurley, Jack Folker, and Dennis Daigle. Thanks go to staff and associates that produced sample panels.

People from various disciplines shared knowledge specifically for the book. Thanks to Jennifer Ayres, Simeon Bankoff, James Biber, Steve Bielitz, Paul Castrucci, Annie Coggan, Ed Cooke, Robert Falk, Bill Finch, Jonathan Foote, Bernard Gallagher, Carrol Griggs, James Hartin, Grayson Jordan, Lloyd Kahn, M. Fine Lumber, Joan Maloof, Eddie O'Donnell, Scott Peltzer, Daniel Rudnitzki, Jennifer Stuart, A. Hays Town Jr., David White, Diana Young, and Carl Zimring.

We are grateful to the many individuals and organizations that assisted with onsite visits for photography. We feel badly that the book could not include more examples of design installations. Thanks to our customers in the business and the range of their design work that the woods have served.

We are thankful to the trees that make a book possible, and also supplied content. Wood reclamation does not save trees in vast numbers. ("Used lumber" amounts to just a fraction of one percent of all wood used in the world.) But reclaimed woods are witness to the beauty and distress of forests and inspire renewal.

And finally, thank you to our families. Parents, brothers, sisters, wives, and children. For their love, support, artistic inspiration, and patience. They're still our first thought when we think of reclamation.

—Alan Solomon and Klaas Armster

Index

Note: Page numbers in *italics* indicate photo captions and/or photos. Page numbers in **bold** indicate main discussions and characteristics of featured wood species.

Captions, pages 1–6

Page 1: Crosscut saw with barn threshing floor.

Page 2: White pine in the Adirondacks. Photograph by Paul Schaefer, c. 1945.

Pages 4–5: Longleaf pine at demolition site, 351 Broadway, New York.

Page 6: Reclaimed woods at Sawkill Lumber Co., Brooklyn.

Designer: Peter Ahlberg
Production Manager: Anet Sirna-Bruder

Library of Congress Control Number: 2018958262

ISBN: 978-1-4197-3818-0
eISBN: 978-1-68335-650-9

Copyright © 2019 Klaas Armster and Alan Solomon

Jacket © 2019 Abrams

Published in 2019 by Abrams, an imprint of ABRAMS. All rights reserved. No portion of this book may be reproduced, stored in a retrieval system, or transmitted in any form or by any means, mechanical, electronic, photocopying, recording, or otherwise, without written permission from the publisher.

Printed and bound in the United States
10 9 8 7 6 5 4 3 2 1

Abrams books are available at special discounts when purchased in quantity for premiums and promotions as well as fundraising or educational use. Special editions can also be created to specification. For details, contact specialsales@abramsbooks.com or the address below.

Abrams® is a registered trademark of Harry N. Abrams, Inc.

ABRAMS
The Art of Books

195 Broadway
New York, NY 10007
abramsbooks.com

Photograph Credits

Michel Arnaud: front cover, 1, 4–5, 6, 8, 10–11, 12, 15, 16, 17, 19 (all), 22–23, 44–45, 46, 50 (all), 51, 53, 54, 55 (bottom left and right), 57, 58, 59, 60, 61, 64, 65 (all), 67, 68, 69, 70–71, 73, 74, 75, 76, 77, 78, 83, 85, 86, 87, 88, 89, 91, 93, 94, 95, 96, 97, 99, 101 (both), 103, 104, 106, 107, 108, 110, 111, 112–113, 115, 116, 117, 119, 120, 121 (both), 123, 124, 125, 126, 127 (both), 128–129, 130, 131, 132, 133, 134–135, 137 (all), 141 (all), 144, 147 (all), 148–149, 150, 152, 154, 156, 157, 158, 159, 160 (both), 161, 162 (all), 163, 164, 165, 166 (all), 167, 168, 169 (both), 182, 183 (both), 192–193, 194, 195 (both), 196 (both), 197, 198, 199, 200, 201, 202, 203, 206, 207, 210, 211, 212, 213 (both), 214, 215, 218–219, 220–221, 222–223, 230, 232–233, 241, back cover.

Additional credits: Alamy: 114; Ball & Albanese: 174, 175; Lincoln Barbour: 176, 177 (all); Berkshire Museum/Google Art Project: 24; Curt Clayton: 178, 179, 180 (both), 181 (all); Brad Dickson: 208, 209; Emily Dryden: 142, 155 (both); Todd Mason: 184–185; Beth Maynor Finch: 224, 226 (second, third, and fourth from left); The Forest History Society: 227; Nicole Franzen: 172–173; Getty Open Content: 34–35, 38, 43; Josh Goleman: 153; Heidi's Bridge: 171, 172; Library of Congress: 14, 32, 37, 47, 49, 52, 55 (top), 56, 62, 63 (both), 72, 79, 80, 81, 82, 90, 92, 100, 118, 122; John Muggenborg: 204, 205 (both); Karl Neumann: 190 (both); Lois Barden Collection/Image by William T. Clarke: 36; Metropolitan Museum of Art: 105; Arthur Nager, 109; Museum of Fine Arts, Boston: 28; National Library of the Netherlands: 27; New York Public Library: 20, 21, 66; NYC Municipal Archives: 228; On-Site Management: 188, 189; OTTO: 186, 187; Park Avenue Armory: 231; Potter County Historical Society: 42; Eric Sloane/Courtesy Charmaine Sloane Thacker: 234 (all); George M. Sutton/Cornell Lab of Ornithology: 226 (left); University of Texas at Arlington Library/The Portal to Texas History: 225; University of Washington Special Collections: 40–41; Saverio Vallauri: 216 (both), 217; Van Cortlandt House Museum: 84.